For the Common Good

For the Common Good

The Ethics of Leadership in the 21st Century

EDITED BY JOHN C. KNAPP

Foreword by Jimmy Carter

Westport, Connecticut
London

Library of Congress Cataloging-in-Publication Data

For the common good: the ethics of leadership in the 21st century / edited by John C. Knapp;
foreword by Jimmy Carter.
    p. cm.
  Includes bibliographical references and index.
  ISBN 0-275-99259-4 (alk. paper)
  1. Leadership—Moral and ethical aspects. I. Knapp, John C. II. Carter, Jimmy, 1924–
HM1261.F67 2007
174—dc22   2006029540

British Library Cataloguing in Publication Data is available.

Library of Congress Catalog Card Number: 2006029540
ISBN: 0-275-99259-4

First published in 2007

Praeger Publishers, 88 Post Road West, Westport, CT 06881
An imprint of Greenwood Publishing Group, Inc.
www.praeger.com

Printed in the United States of America

∞™

The paper used in this book complies with the
Permanent Paper Standard issued by the National
Information Standards Organization (Z39.48-1984).

10 9 8 7 6 5 4 3 2 1

This volume is published in honor of

Betty L. Siegel

*whose twenty-five-year tenure
as president of
Kennesaw State University
exemplified leadership
"for the common good."
The following lines, written
in her honor for this
volume, are by the poet
David Whyte.*

I Am Thinking of Women

(For Betty Siegel)

I am thinking of women of nobility
and purpose, the way they catch the light
and magnetize a crowd, the way men
of individual power standing outside
that gravity well of relational desire
are helpless before the tide, and I think
of them especially, when I think of Yeats,
walking innocently into a room in Dublin
and falling for that woman
haloed in spring light who stood, head high
by a vase of fresh apple blossom
and how then, he pursued her, writing

I will find out where she has gone
And kiss her lips and take her hands
and how he put her into plays depicting
the history of a country struggling to be born
sometimes casting her as a young girl
sometimes as the older woman
who struggles in at last to save the past
from itself and all the while
in love with her from tip to toe
she refused him in marriage
five or six times through the years
so he had to write her
larger and larger in the mind of a nation
to make some good
of the not to be borne, close-in loss.

These women, half enticing, half frightening
these noble profiles imperiously caught,
creating, under the outward stylish drama
cradles of competency, these Maudes,
Eleanors, Indiras, and Elizabeths, sailing
on and above the fray, into present time,
over the surge of history, putting together
whole worlds, universities, conversations, new nations.
They stand in our minds so completely now
some frightening simplicity at their center,
some impatience with that outward show,
we imagine them, suddenly, placed in an ordinary life,
all outward help withdrawn, standing in rags
at the corner, starting blithely again,
with a first helpless stranger
the talk for which they were born,
we see them issuing the first unstoppable invitation,
arranging the welcome shelter from selfishness,
broaching that first beautiful and beckoning
uncertainty, outlining the emerging and finally,
inescapable understanding,
the one that ends with changing the world.
—*David Whyte*

Contents

Foreword

*As we face changes and challenges, we need to hold on to the things that don't
change, the foundations on which we can build our lives despite the uncertainty
and danger of the future.*[1]

I wrote those words just before the dawn of the present century, unaware
of just how challenging the next decade would be for America and the
world. Global terrorism, war, political unrest and natural disasters remind us
daily that ours is indeed a time of uncertainty and danger.

The early 21st century is a moment in history that calls for a new kind of
leadership, capable of addressing complex, global problems while holding
fast to the timeless values our faith and experience have shown us are essential to a good society. Such leadership requires what I have called *social
courage*—the strength of character to rise above political and societal pressures in order to serve the common good of humanity.

In this volume, you will read about trends that are changing our world in
ways we can hardly imagine. The opening chapter by analyst Erik Peterson
predicts that the next two decades will be a period of revolutionary change in
population, conflict, resources, technology, information and economic development. As these sobering trends reshape global society, one conclusion is
inescapable: their combined effects will be to deepen the divide between rich
and poor in our world. Today, as 10 percent of us consume 56 percent of the
world's resources, one-half of the global population struggles to subsist on
less than $2 a day, often lacking clean water, adequate sanitation, basic nour-
ishment, and access to health care and education.[2]

Shortly before the close of the 20th century, I was asked to give a speech answering the question of what I considered to be the world's greatest challenge in the new millennium. I did not have to ponder the question long, for in my experience at The Carter Center—whether in resolving political conflict or working to eradicate diseases—it has been increasingly clear to me that the widening chasm between the world's wealthy and its desperately poor is a genuine threat to *all* people.

So what kind of leadership is required to meet such a challenge? In these pages, John Knapp has assembled a distinguished group of leaders who offer thoughtful responses to this question as they discuss a variety of timely concerns. Not surprisingly, they say that tomorrow's leaders must be collaborative, resourceful and able to see problems from a global perspective. But more important, they share a conviction that leadership *for the common good* is both an ethical imperative and a practical necessity in the face of our uncertain future. Their views are well worth reading.

I am delighted that this book is dedicated to Betty Siegel on the occasion of her retirement after 25 years as president of Kennesaw State University. Rosalynn and I have counted Betty and her husband, Joel, among our friends for many years. As the nation's longest-serving female president of a university, she was a visionary leader who guided a small four-year college to become a leading university with seven colleges, 55 undergraduate and graduate degree programs, and nearly 19,000 students from 120 countries.

This special book is a fitting tribute to Betty Siegel, who has tirelessly promoted the idea that institutions of higher learning have a duty to provide moral leadership in society. In her final year as a president, she invited a group of her peers to gather at the University of Oxford, a place of significant symbolism and historic meaning for today's universities. Over a five-day period, university leaders from across the United States crafted a declaration of beliefs and ethical principles to guide them in using their resources and influence to more effectively address the challenges threatening 21st-century society.

We must hope that this vision will be shared not only by university presidents, but also by leaders in business, government, health care, and other vital institutions, all of which must do their part in providing leadership for the common good.

—*Jimmy Carter*

Introduction

This is a book about the future. In these pages you will explore the ethical requirements of leadership in a century that is already witnessing faster, more sweeping change than any period in human history.

It is also a book about the past. You will read first-hand accounts by several remarkable leaders whose own lives in the late 20th century helped set an enduring standard for good leadership. Their wisdom, together with personal recollections of exemplary leaders like Mahatma Gandhi and Peter Drucker, serves to ground our discussion of the future in the hard-earned lessons of the recent past.

Most of us today take it for granted that our world is changing and will change even more dramatically in the decades ahead. But that was not so for people living at the turn of previous centuries. "Our forebears expected the future to be pretty much like their present, which had been pretty much like their past," observes artificial intelligence pioneer Ray Kurzweil.[3] How many of our great-grandparents had an inkling of what the 20th century would bring?

In his incisive book, *Humanity: A Moral History of the Twentieth Century*, Jonathan Glover writes, "At the start of the century there was optimism, coming from the Enlightenment, that the spread of a humane and scientific outlook would lead to the fading away, not only of war, but of other forms of cruelty and barbarism."[4] Of course, we now know that it was a short-lived season of hope, yielding all too soon to the brutality that was to mark the bloodiest century in human history.

The opening years of the 21st century have witnessed no such naiveté. The millennium awoke to terrorists in New York, Washington, London and

Madrid; greedy criminals in corporate boardrooms; famine, genocide and an AIDS epidemic in Africa; deadly floods in Asia and America; new nuclear threats from unstable despots; and the uncertainties of globalization in a world we were told was "flat" after all. Yet even with our generation's knowledge and expectations, Kurzweil warns, "the future will be far more surprising than most observers realize: few have truly internalized the implications of the fact that the rate of change itself is accelerating."

One who fully grasps the magnitude of this is Erik Peterson, director of the Global Strategy Institute at the Center for Strategic & International Studies, whose sobering chapter, "Scanning More Distant Horizons," is our first chapter. He paints a vivid picture of the stormy waters 21st-century leaders will be called upon to navigate, describing seven revolutionary trends that already are redefining global society. Are leaders prepared for the upheaval to come? "In my view the conclusion is as inescapable as it is uncomfortable," he warns. "Across the layers of social organization— government, business, civil society, academia, and elsewhere—we are mired in pervasive short-termism precisely at the time when we need to be more forward-looking. The stakes are profound."

LEADERSHIP FOR THE COMMON GOOD

Few people would disagree with the proposition that good leadership is more crucial than ever, especially as it is increasingly apparent that our collective future depends in very large measure on the actions and priorities of the few who lead powerful institutions. But we also know that *good* leadership requires more than just effectiveness in getting things done. It is as much about who leaders *are* as what they do. And it is about the ends they value and the means they choose to pursue them.

The chapters that follow are concerned principally with what may be called *the ethics of leadership*—that is, the obligations of leaders to promote justice, fairness, trust, and the conditions necessary for people to live well in communities that flourish. We have chosen to attend to practical matters in these writings, leaving the dissection of leadership theory to others. It is our hope that the trenchant insights and diverse backgrounds of those who have collaborated to produce this volume will contribute to a much-needed public discussion of these issues among people of all cultures.

Ethics involves many things, but it is primarily concerned with understanding and achieving human well-being, especially in the context of our relationships with one another. The ultimate aim of ethical action may be seen as what Aristotle called "the common good of all." He recognized, as we do, that there are differences of opinion about what is good, and about which goods are best for all concerned. But this is precisely why he thought the matter deserved serious discussion. In our time, it is the task of leaders to invite this discussion and work with others to formulate a vision of the common good might finally bridge the political, social, and economic chasms that divide us.

We must have no illusions about the difficulty of this task. Indeed, as David Hollenbach has said, "the idea of the common good is in trouble today—serious trouble." This loss of hope flows from contemporary assumptions about the fragmentation of our cultural landscape. "Pluralism, by definition, means people disagree about what the good life is, so if we respect their freedom, there seems little possibility of attaining a shared understanding of a common good." Yet the idea may find new life as globalization increases interdependency and technology forges new linkages between disparate peoples. In Hollenbach's words,

> The pursuit of the global common good thus has social, intellectual, and institutional dimensions. It calls for a social struggle to move the patterns of global interdependence away from domination and toward reciprocity based on equality. It requires intellectual commitment to listening as well as speaking in a genuine dialogue with those who are different. And it calls for transformation of the institutional centers of decision-making in our increasingly interconnected globe. In theological terms, it calls us to seek a world of greater communion. [5]

If the world were to agree on a vision of the common good, what might it be? Frances Hesselbein argues that to some extent such a vision already exists, one that "embraces healthy children, strong families, good schools, decent housing, and work that dignifies, all in the cohesive, inclusive society that cares about all its people." There can be little disagreement that this is "the dream that lies before us," she insists, but we must be realistic about how hard it will be to accomplish, especially when extended to a global community wracked by poverty, disease, hunger, war and injustice. It is certain that governments cannot do it alone; therefore, "great corporate leaders . . . religious leaders, university and college presidents, and the leaders of voluntary organizations need to add their vision and voices to the leadership effort."[6]

GOOD LEADERS IN THE 21st CENTURY

So just what is it that will distinguish *good* leaders in the 21st century? Erik Peterson begins Chapter 1 with the words of Gandhi, who calls all of us to "be the change" we want to see in the world. His chapter does much to illuminate the scope of transformation leadership must yet undergo, providing a clear-eyed analysis of the global condition of humanity and how it is being radically altered by several trends. Hunger, environmental degradation, warfare, and disease are among the looming threats, not only to the most vulnerable populations but also to the common good of all. He concludes, "Our overarching challenge is to provide the knowledge for leaders to develop vision, to inculcate them with the understanding to execute on their vision, and to help them develop a conceptual and ethical foundation on which difficult—sometimes, excruciating—trade-offs will have to be made." He worries, however, that leadership is "being replaced by management, strategy by tactics, long-term planning by triage reactions, principle by expediency, and far-sighted vision by mere management by the numbers."

In Chapter 2, Lynn Barendsen and Howard Gardner ask, "What are the traits of good leaders across time and how do these leaders adjust to rapidly changing times?" To answer this, they draw from their own primary research with leaders and from the examples of successful role models, including the late John Gardner, an influential leader and often-consulted expert on the subject. Their conclusion: good leaders are highly committed to three things: excellence, ethics and engagement. Throughout their chapter, they provide helpful case examples of leaders who maintain these commitments in the face of globalization and market pressures. But they also point to the scarcity of such leaders. One, perhaps surprising, role model is the world-class cellist Yo Yo Ma who "does not worry about globalization, but instead, shows us how it can diversify and deepen our cultural understandings." He is an example for all leaders by being "fully engaged in his music, and equally engaged in his service of others."

Each of our contributors shows how the changing context for leadership calls for changes in leaders themselves. No place is this more true than the arena of public opinion, where a growing chorus of critics demands constant accountability and puts leaders to the test in ways their predecessors never imagined. The third chapter looks at this phenomenon and the attendant deficit of trust in institutions and their leaders—a disturbing and deepening worldwide problem. The implication is that 21st-century leaders must develop new skills and higher degrees of emotional intelligence in order to maintain necessary relationships with the range of diverse stakeholders whose interests intersect with their own. Emotional intelligence involves both social awareness and self-awareness; the latter requiring a measure of personal humility not always encouraged or rewarded by business and government institutions.

A more personal account is found in Chapter 4, where Frances Hesselbein offers wise insights about leadership in a warm tribute to the late Peter Drucker, her close friend and the 20th century's foremost expert on management. She is, of course, a distinguished leader in her own right—serving as the highly successful CEO of the Girl Scouts of America, mentoring and teaching the top brass of the U.S. Army, and receiving the Presidential Medal of Freedom, the nation's highest civilian honor. She reminds us of Drucker's maxim, "Leadership cannot be taught, but it can be learned," even as she repeats her own adage, "Leadership is about how to be, not how to do." Ultimately, the aim of leadership must be the common good, for all leaders need to accept responsibility not just for their own institutions, but also for what Drucker called "the community as a whole."

The second section of the book considers the ethics of leadership in the daunting contexts of global conflict, environmental degradation and malnutrition. We begin with a chapter by Nobel Peace Prize laureate John Hume, the great peacemaker of Northern Ireland. He acknowledges, "we are living through one of the greatest revolutions in the history of the world," yet he is nonetheless optimistic that as transport, technology and telecommunications make the planet smaller, "we are in a stronger position to shape that world." In his view, 21st-century leaders have a better opportunity than those of any earlier generation to put an end to war and major conflict. Laying out a set of principles for this process, he proposes that the United States' original motto, *E Pluribus Unum* ("out of many, we are one"), might someday be "a summary of the philosophy of the entire world." His conclusion calls for the European Union and the United States to form a "permanent international body" to promote global dialog and resolve conflicts.

Arun Gandhi is the grandson of Mahatma Gandhi, from whom he learned many of life's lessons as a child. In the sixth chapter, he describes the principles of self-discipline and nonviolence that leaders must embody in order to reduce the intensity of conflict in a dangerous world. Discussing some lessons of India's history, he shows the consequences of ethical compromise and stresses that successful leaders "must be wedded to a high standard of ethics and morality." Rich with personal anecdotes, his chapter includes an illuminating account of the childhood experiences that formed his legendary grandfather's character as a leader. What he learned about love, respect, compassion, understanding, and acceptance may be even more essential for 21st-century leaders.

No serious effort to cope with global change could be undertaken without the active involvement of business leaders. Yet it is they who are often vilified by leaders in government, education, and the social sector for their roles in environmental, human rights and other problems. Can leaders in business be brought to the table as equal partners in a collaborative pursuit of the common good? Ray Anderson not only thinks so, he has found himself at the head of the table as co-chair of the President's Council on Sustainable Development. His inspiring story, found in Chapter 7, demonstrates the power of one visionary leader to make a meaningful difference and blaze a trail for others to follow. The founder of a billion-dollar manufacturing company with factories on four continents, a late-life epiphany brought him to grips with the harmful environmental impact of his company. Since that time he has led an initiative to neutralize his company's effects on the environment, create a model of sustainability for industry, and turn his 5,000-employee firm into an "*eco-system, in which cooperation replaces confrontation*, and one that includes Earth in win-win-win relationships." His chapter also sounds a dire warning about the harm that will be suffered by future generations if industrial leaders fail to wake up to long-term consequences of their practices.

The environmental crisis is not unrelated to the problem of feeding the world's hungry, as E. T. York shows in Chapter 8. Internationally known for more than 40 years as an advocate of solutions to hunger and malnutrition, he declares this to be "the great moral challenge of our generation." He draws on his deep experience as a researcher and advisor to six U.S. presidents to make a compelling case that global hunger can be alleviated with the help of advances in science, technology, and agriculture—but only if leaders have the will and moral vision to make it happen.

It is not coincidental that E. T. York is also chancellor emeritus of the University System of Florida, for higher education is as indispensable to solving the problem of hunger as it is to addressing every other issue raised in these pages. Erik Peterson contends that *only* higher education is positioned to "ask how we develop our leaders, how we condition their thinking, what their moral and ethical frameworks are, and what priorities for action are being contemplated." For this reason, the last section of this book explores the roles, responsibilities, and untapped potential of higher education as a locus of thought leadership and a developer of good leaders for future society. If there is anything common to today's leaders across virtually all sectors, it is a university education.

But are universities prepared to embrace this opportunity? And are they able? Beheruz Sethna takes up these questions in Chapter 9. As president of the University of West Georgia and the first immigrant of Indian origin to lead a university in the United States, he sees an "awesome responsibility" for universities: "We have the opportunity to influence 18 million young (and not so young) minds and help them obtain the tools for ethical leadership in

America—and, because America still is in a leadership position in world higher education—in the world." Echoing our theme that good leadership begins with who leaders are, rather than what they do, he argues that the primary mission of universities is "*changing lives*," rather than the traditional triumvirate of teaching, research and service. He does not flinch from acknowledging the difficulty of this mission, and ends his chapter with a call for his peers to "embrace that duty, that challenge, and that responsibility."

Yet even if university leaders rise to the challenge, they cannot succeed by going it alone. Therefore, Chapter 10 examines the imperative for institutions to collaborate across sectors in order to tackle complex, global problems that are beyond the reach of any one discipline or sector. David and Michael Siegel, both scholars who study higher education leadership, believe collaboration is often resisted because it "complicates conventional understandings of place and purpose." Using the higher education enterprise as a fulcrum, they identify key features of multisector collaborations, address some of the problems inherent in them, and consider the changing role of leadership and leaders in such undertakings. In their words, "A greater sense of mindfulness and attentiveness in the development of cross-sector collaborations—a conscientious attempt to know as we wish to be known—would benefit the process immeasurably and ultimately create a more symbiotic connection—literally and figuratively—among the vast maze of pipelines."

Our final chapter brings us back to the words of Gandhi that open Chapter 1. Lawrence Carter's chapter on the development of future leaders is entitled, "Global Ethical Leadership and Higher Education: 'Being the Change You Wish to See.'" As dean of the Martin Luther King Jr. Chapel at Morehouse College, he has a passionate interest in the formation of leaders who are "spiritually aware visionary activists." For examples, he points to Gandhi, King, and Daisaku Ikeda, the Japanese philosopher, educator and social activist who said, "What our world most requires now is the kind of education that fosters love for human kind, that develops character, that provides an intellectual basis for the realization of peace and empowers learners to contribute to improve society." The chapter concludes with the declaration of the Oxford Conclave on Global Ethics, a statement by university leaders calling for the transformation of universities to make them more effective agents for the transformation of society.

A CLOSING WORD

It has been a rare privilege to work with the distinguished group of thinkers and leaders brought together by this project. That all are friends of

Betty Siegel, to whom this volume is dedicated, is a testament to the extent of her influence and her passion for educating ethical leaders. Howard Gardner may have best expressed our collective regard for this very special woman: "When significant American educational leaders of the last quarter century are listed, Betty Siegel will be in that select company. And when the list is trimmed to those leaders who are innovative, ethical and spirited, there will be a special place for Betty Siegel."

We are more convinced now than when this project began that the extraordinary challenges of the 21st century call for nothing less than ethically astute leaders capable of, and fully committed to, seeking the common good of all. It is our hope that this collection of chapters might contribute something of value to those who heed this call.

—*John C. Knapp*
Atlanta, Georgia

SECTION I
THE NEW CLIMATE FOR LEADERSHIP

CHAPTER 1

Scanning More Distant Horizons

Erik R. Peterson

Nearly a half century ago, Mahatma Gandhi said that "[y]ou must be the change you want to see in the world." Gandhi's words certainly represented—and continue to represent—a call to action for those concerned with ethical leadership across all layers of social organization. As we move further into the 21st century, amidst ever more profound change taking place ever more rapidly, his words should resonate with leaders and followers alike even more than at the time when they were spoken.

Before we can meet Gandhi's challenge, however, we need to identify the nature of the change we want to see in the world. Here there is certainly no art in pinpointing the big, overarching challenges of our era. The majority are painfully well documented and well understood. We live in a world in which a large chunk of humanity has insufficient access to even the most basic of needs, such as food and water. Large populations are deprived of basic human rights and economic opportunity. Massive stratifications—economic, social, and gender, among others—continue to afflict large segments across geographical regions. Obscene numbers of children do not have the health care and educational opportunities that their peers elsewhere take for granted. Environmental degradation, as massive as it now is, is accelerating. Poor governance systems are imposing monumental social and economic opportunity costs on their populations. Warfare, terrorism, and crime continue to cloud the futures of communities, countries, and regions.

Defining an interdisciplinary and appropriately scaled approach to these issues, necessarily, is significantly more challenging. How does one assign priorities when addressing any single one of these challenges would mean an improved livelihood for large numbers of people, and when passing another

challenge would condemn the affected segment to the continuation of its
affliction?[1] Most challenging of all, however, is pounding out a collective
approach to improving the predicament of humanity—the common good.
In that regard, the effort in 2000 at the United Nations to delineate the UN
Millennium Development Goals (MDGs) out to the year 2015 was a vitally
important and worthwhile exercise. At once, it provided a snapshot of the
present situation and a trajectory against which we can measure our collective progress as well as assess conditions region by region.[2]

But substantially more needs to be done. From my perspective, it is bitterly
disappointing that in this age of instantaneous communication, of information ubiquity, and of global data flows, so little serious and sustained attention is devoted to identifying and then prioritizing our approach to
addressing these kinds of challenges. Likewise, it is disappointing that so few
organizations are seeking to develop—or, for that matter, even explore—
innovative and interdisciplinary approaches to prepositioning for the world
to come. In my view the conclusion is as inescapable as it is uncomfortable:
Across the layers of social organization—government, business, civil society,
academia, and elsewhere—we are mired in pervasive short-termism precisely at the time when we need to be more forward-looking. The stakes are
profound.

Why are we so handcuffed by the near term? A number of factors are
contributing to this dilemma. In the political sphere, too often the election
process limits the capacity of leaders to look forward. Typically, in democracies new election campaigns begin before the last ones have transpired.
Necessarily, this skews thinking by leaders to the present and offers little by
way of incentive to policies or actions that unfold after election terms have
ended. In the business sphere, the pressure of quarterly profit statements
and the remarkable pressure of second-to-second fluctuations in stock prices
skew the capacity of the majority of leaders to look to the longer term. Even
nongovernmental organizations (NGOs) and academic leaders find themselves hamstrung by the gravity of the present.

In order to contemplate the requirements for leadership in the 21st century,
leadership that we hope and trust will lead to an improvement of the common
good, a fundamental shift in culture will be necessary. To give effect to
Gandhi's observation, in order for us to engage the more distant future, we
need to think in ever more innovative terms about what kinds of forces are
shaping our world and what we can be doing now to influence those forces. If
the signs of our collective failure of principled leadership are clear in the nature
and scope of the predicaments that humanity now faces, they will be all the
more obvious if we fail to act in the meantime.

Predictions of the future are elusive by their very nature. How, then, should we organize our thinking and action on the longer-term challenges we confront? My view is that we can begin to approximate the more distant horizon by examining seven critical drivers of change that together help to demarcate the complex set of opportunities and threats that lie ahead.

DEMOGRAPHIC DYNAMICS

The obvious starting point is to assess trends in the area of population. In this regard, we now stand at a remarkable threshold with respect to sheer numbers, the urban–rural balance of our population, the inland–coastal positioning of our populations and cities, the age composition of our societies, the rate of growth, and the pattern of migration flows. Together, these factors will have a remarkable effect on economic development and opportunity in regions across the planet. Beyond that, they will have a profound impact on stability and security within countries and across regions.

It is remarkable that the global population has risen from 4.5 billion in 1981 to its current level of more than 6.5 billion. The latest projections from the United Nations suggest that our numbers will continue to grow significantly—to 7.9 billion by 2025 and to 9.1 billion by the year 2050. Roughly speaking, that means we are now growing at a rate of 77 million people each year, 8,700 every hour, 146 people every minute, and nearly 2.5 people every single second. As daunting as these numbers may seem, however, we should note that they represent an improvement—in fact, a pronounced improvement—from the kinds of forecasts of exponential population growth that we saw in the 1970s and the early 1980s. The latest indications from the United National Population Division suggest that under the moderate scenario, in which we see the continuation of declines in growth levels, the global population could stabilize in the 2070s in the lower nine billions.

If the UN's projections prove to be correct, that clearly would be a major inflection point. In the meantime, though, a number of other important thresholds in the area of population will be passed. The first and most immediate will be in 2007, when the number of people living in urban areas will exceed the number of rural dwellers for the first time ever.[3] The number of people living on coasts is also expected to rise significantly—from 3.2 billion in 2004 to a projected 6.2 billion in the year 2025.[4] Moreover, a large number of the world's largest cities will fall in this category. In light of the tragic developments on our own Gulf Coast in 2005 with Hurricane Katrina, it takes little by way of imagination to envisage what this heightened vulnerability might imply.

Another critical dimension of future change in the area of population is the aging of many societies, particularly in what we now call the "developed" world. This trend does not lend itself to the identification of specific inflection points, but we can anticipate that by the middle of the century the number of older (older than 60 years) will exceed the number of young (less than 60) for the first time in history. In the meantime, the number of older persons as a percentage of total population can be expected to rise significantly in a number of countries, particularly in Asia and Europe. The data on median age tell the story. In Europe, the median age was 29.9 years in 1950; it has increased to 37.6 by the year 2000 and is expected to continue rising to 47.1 by 2050. In Japan, the corresponding figure in 1950 was 22.3; by 2050, according to projections, it will be more than twice that level (52.3 years).

To broaden our analysis of future population trends, we need to superimpose on these elements another critical factor: the breadth of high-growth versus negative-growth countries is getting wider and wider. The lion's share of the absolute growth that we can expect to see in the world will occur in a relatively small number of countries, many situated in the Middle East and sub-Saharan Africa, with limited capacities to accommodate such growth. Some face the prospect of a tripling of their populations in the next 45 years alone. By contrast, at the other end of the age spectrum, a number of states are encountering a range of challenges associated with depopulation. All in all, more than 50 countries face the prospect that their populations will stabilize or even shrink out through the middle of the century. Some current assessments of demographic trends suggest, for example, that the Russian Federation is currently depopulating at alarming rates—perhaps by as much as 100 people each hour. Another example is Japan, which may have reached its population apogee in 2004; the 2005 Japanese census revealed that the population was 19,000 lower than the prior year. To varying extents, these countries face profound uncertainties about worker to retiree ratios, the composition of future workforces, maintaining social welfare systems, and other more general pressures—for example, political competition—between young and old.

At the time of this writing, the strains in Europe over clashes of culture, religion, and opportunity between immigrant groups and traditional populations are manifesting themselves in ways that may reveal future challenges. The current circumstances in Europe may be a precursor of even higher levels of tension in the future, as we project migration as a means of normalizing the respective pressures in negative-growth countries, on the one hand, and high-growth countries, on the other. The most recent projections from the United Nations suggest that out to the year 2050, some 100 million people will migrate to another country.[5]

When we consider these elements of population change—aggregate trends, balance between urban and rural and interior and coastline, age composition, and the widening dispersion in rates of growth—the conclusions are profound. These factors will influence the nature of economic activity, the rate of economic growth, propensities in consumption, savings, and investment, the volume and directions of capital flows within countries and across borders, and fiscal and monetary policies. Beyond that, they will have a pronounced impact on stability and security in regions across the world.

MANAGEMENT OF KEY RESOURCES

In looking forward, we also need to assess our capacity to satisfy growing global demand in a number of important areas including food, water, and energy. To do this, the uncomfortable starting point is the proposition that our current resource-related predicaments, daunting as they are, are likely to become all the more challenging in the future. Current estimates suggest that we live in a world in which more than 800 million people are seriously undernourished. Ten preschool-age children die each minute from malnutrition.[6] In the area of water, analysts believe that some 1.1 billion people do not have access to safe drinking water and that 2.6 billion people have inadequate sanitation. The United Nations projects that the number of affected people could rise to 3 billion by the year 2025. In energy, the last two years have punctuated the frailties in the global supply–demand calculus, the susceptibility of the structure to shocks from both natural disaster and human activity, and price volatility.

The prospect of serious dislocation arising from widening supply–demand gaps in all three of these areas could lead to even higher levels of stratification and instability. Leaders cannot discount such a possibility.

If the level of undernourishment is high and could increase, what are the factors to explain why we are falling behind in the first MDG, which would reduce by one-half the proportion of people across the world whose income is less than a single dollar per day? The first factor that we need to take into account is mounting pressure on agricultural production from population growth. As suggested above, the correlation between high population growth and the inability of countries to accommodate such growth suggests that population is an especially important obstacle to reversing hunger. On the supply side, the operative question is the extent to which agricultural producers can lift production to meet anticipated demand. Here, technology and other shifts in productivity are wildcards. A third variable is poor governance—or in some cases, the lack of governance as manifested, for instance, in instability or conflict. Resource input availability, in particular water, is another important factor. Finally, and certainly a tremendously significant variable, is environmental degradation. Desertification, deforestation, overuse, and other human practices raise profound uncertainties about our capacity to expand arable land areas.

When expressed globally, our track record in meeting agricultural targets has been mixed. Progress has been extremely uneven. Although the percentage of total world population suffering from chronic hunger has declined, the reality is that the absolute numbers have increased. The United Nations estimates that the number of hungry people in the world declined from 824 million in 1990 to 815 million in 2002.[7] Although it is far too modest, the overall levels reflect both remarkable improvements and disappointing setbacks. On the improvements side, Eastern Asia succeeded in reducing the number of persons with insufficient food by 47 million, South-Eastern Asia by 12 million, and Latin America and the Caribbean by 7 million. In contrast, Western Asia added 8 million to its number of hungry, Southern Asia 15 million, and sub-Saharan Africa 34 million.[8] Recent projections suggest that the total number could grow by another 100 million by the year 2015.[9]

Reducing malnutrition across our planet, or at the very least reducing the level of undernourishment to MDG target levels, will be a reflection of our capacity to expand production, improve distribution (especially to rural poor), ramp up governance, and mobilize technologies that can improve production efficiencies. In the face of relentless increases in population, that will require much more by way of a concerted international effort than is now apparent.

It is striking that agricultural production accounts for an estimated 70 percent of our use of the planet's fresh water. Roughly a quarter of our use of fresh water goes in support of manufacturing and industry, and the remaining amount—about 8 percent—is used by cities, towns, and municipalities. The upshot is that water will be a critical constraint not only to agriculture but also to basic human health, economic development, and stability and security.

The UN Environmental Program notes that consumption of fresh water rose sixfold globally from 1900 to 1995, more than twice as fast as the human population; furthermore, it notes that one-third of the world's population now lives in "water-stressed" areas and by 2025 that number could rise to two out of every three people.[10] By 2025, we can expect to see global shortfalls of water equal to 2,000 cubic kilometers—that is the equivalent to the annual flow of 10 Nile Rivers . . . or 110 Colorado Rivers.[11] The breadth of the water challenge is staggering. There are a number of acute symptoms. Water tables are falling, sometimes precipitously, in regions stretching from

Asia to the United States. Major rivers ranging from the Yellow River to the Ganges to the Colorado River are no longer consistently reaching the ocean. Many large inland lakes—from the Aral Sea to Lake Chad—are disappearing rapidly.

In early 2005, the UN Committee on Sustainable Development suggested that in order to meet the projected demand for water through the middle of the century, the challenge before us all is to double the supply of fresh water. After that time, according to the Commission, some 50 percent more water will be needed with each successive generation. It is an open question how—or even if—we will be able to satisfy this kind of projected demand. For all these reasons, we can expect water to become an ever more "strategic" resource. The bottom line here is that how effectively we address the challenge of international water—how well we can manage supply, demand, quality, and distribution—will mean the difference between life and death, between health and disease, and between stability and instability in key regions across the planet. Billions of lives across the planet will be affected by how well we manage to manage the strategic challenge of water.

The third critical resource is energy. International linkages through energy have been more than apparent since the oil embargo of the early 1970s, and the more recent global supply–demand shocks brought about by simultaneous instability in oil-producing countries across the planet underline that the situation is little changed today. There is good reason to anticipate that volatilities associated with energy will be even more pronounced in the future.

In this area, the projections of the future are as significant for what will *not* change as for the change we can anticipate. First, our capacity to shift away from hydrocarbons in global energy consumption will be considerably more difficult than many of us would like to accept. Most long-term energy forecasts from international organizations, national governments, and industry agree that the current high level of reliance on fossil fuels (oil, natural gas, and coal) will persist well through the year 2020 and beyond. They generally concur that fossil fuels will maintain more than an 85 percent share of global energy consumption through the year 2030, that alternative fuels will maintain their current share of about 8 percent, and that the share of nuclear energy will fall in relative terms to about 3 to 4 percent. Furthermore, they generally indicate that fossil fuels will also account for 80 percent of the growth in energy demand in the longer term. At issue is our lack of ability to effect a rapid substitution of renewable energy sources for hydrocarbons. We face an extremely complicated set of challenges involving the current economics of energy source, the costs of retrofitting large energy infrastructures, and scale issues that limit the capacity of renewable energy sources to substitute rapidly.

The second dimension of the energy challenges that is not likely to change is the dependence of the world on the Organization of Petroleum Exporting Countries (OPEC) for its hydrocarbon resources. The OECD's *World Energy Outlook 2004* suggests that OPEC as a source of global oil consumption may exceed the 50 percent level by the year 2025.[12] Within OPEC, the Middle East and North Africa (MENA) share of hydrocarbon production will steadily increase. In its current reference scenario, the OECD is projecting that MENA's share of world oil production will rise from 35 percent in 2004 to 44 percent in the year 2030.[13]

The broader conclusions associated with these two "non-changes" are inescapable. Despite the fact that we would like to see more rapid substitution of renewable alternatives to hydrocarbon, despite the fact that we would like to see a decline in import dependencies in the United States and in other major energy-consuming countries, despite the fact that developed and developing countries alike would benefit from more stable and security energy markets, and despite the fact that we would like to see a reversal of the economic degradation brought about by consumption of hydrocarbons, we appear to be moving toward a "more-of-the-same" future. An abrupt and significant change of our energy pathway into the future would imply political and social adjustments that appear to be beyond the pale of the possible.

If these are the things that we can expect not to change on the more distant horizons, then what will the most significant elements to change the current world energy predicament? By far, the biggest change we can anticipate is an explosion of demand—by more than 50 percent through the year 2030— driven primarily by the developing world, driven within the developing world by Asia, and driven within Asia by China. This surge in demand, inexorably, will test the capacity of consumer countries to moderate their increases in demand, the capacity of producing states to increase production capacities to meet demand, and the capacity of all countries to weather continued rounds of geopolitical, economic, and price volatilities that are attendant with such significant increases in demand and potential supply–demand dislocations.

The operative questions that we must now face is: Can producers expand their production to meet these anticipated increases in demand? James Schlesinger, whose policy experience and command of the full range of energy-related (as well as other) issues is legendary, sums things up in a recent article entitled "Thinking Seriously About Energy and Oil's Future" in which he argues that:

> The implications are clear. Even present trends are unsustainable. Sometime in the decades ahead, the world will no longer be able to accommodate rising energy demand with increased production of conventional oil.[14]

The broader implications of this potential collapsing bubble in energy are enormous. First, we will have to redraw the map of the geopolitics of energy. The current calculus will yield, day by day, to a new framework in which new economic powers with mega-populations such as China and India continue to recast the demand side of the equation. We are already witnessing a new dimension of relations between Beijing and Delhi on how to manage their competition for energy. On the supply side, the capacity of producers to bring new resources online—for example, Caspian Sea and West Africa—will be instrumental to answering whether the period ahead will be somewhat stable or whether producers and consumers alike are vectored toward a period of acute instability.

As we contemplate how to preposition ourselves for the future, it is striking how little we understand the complex linkages between these strategic resources. Agriculture, as mentioned, draws some 70 percent of our fresh water. It follows that practices aimed at reducing that use of water—by reducing evaporation, lining irrigation canals to reduce leakage, implementing drip irrigation, and so on—could help reduce the pressures on fresh water. At the same time, we need to be vigilant to the potential for cascading effects of collapsing bubbles in each of these resources. They are all so very integrally linked that an abrupt shift in one may generate secondary effects on the others.

Obviously, our stewardship of all three of these critical resources—food, water, and energy—had monumental implications for the welfare and prosperity of the human family and the capacity of the planet to carry our population. Each of these resources will represent a test for leadership. It will not only be a function of "thinking seriously" about future prospects, as James Schlesinger succinctly describes it in the context of energy. It will also involve "acting seriously," especially before critical thresholds are reached and the consequences of inaction or misguided action serve to exacerbate the problems. This implies surmounting political and other barriers to actions informed by the most efficient approaches to meeting these resource challenges.

TECHNOLOGICAL INNOVATION AND DIFFUSION

The horizon in scientific and technological innovation is by definition difficult to scan as a result of the remarkably wide spectrum of current progress and the equally remarkable complexities associated with the convergence of various technological breakthroughs. From my perspective, however, three broad areas suggest the potential to be significant drivers of change into the more distant future. Each of these areas will generate significant positive effects, but each will also confront leaders with the need to make ever more complex decisions on ever shorter timeframes.

Computation is the first area in which we can continue to anticipate significant advances. Clearly, this is an area that is changing by the day. On one hand, we need to think in terms of deep computing—our capacity to enable modeling and other computational applications on ever-greater scales with machines with ever-greater speeds. The achievement this year of operations above the 280-teraflop level by the Blue Gene L computer at the Laurence Livermore Laboratories represented a step change over earlier advances.[15] In the future, we can look to continued advances in the computation speeds and capabilities of supercomputers; it is a question of when, not if, the quadrillion operations per second level is shattered in the next few years.

On the other hand, we can also anticipate continued revolutionary advances in the area of pervasive computing—the continuation of the infusion of computation in nearly every facet of our everyday lives. Many of us are coming to understand intuitively that computation is integrating into the totality of our way of being. The rapidly growing capacities of both governments and private organizations to gather, organize, cross-check, synthesize, analyze, and generate products on billions and billions of fragments of information is pushing into a new era. Such a period will be characterized by the benefits of such heightened information awareness. In contrast, the dangers implicit with such concentrations of information are self-evident. The recent breaches of security among a number of corporations have served to demonstrate the very considerable risks associated with these dramatically expanded computational capabilities.

A second key driver of longer-range change in this area is *biotechnology and genomics*. Humanity is on countdown now for a number of biotechnical discoveries and innovations that will follow the completion of the Human Genome Project. Such discoveries could—and likely will—have a dramatic effect on our health and well being. They suggest the potential that our children will lead longer and healthier lives, and that health care can be transformed from its current "one-size-fits-all" approach to a phase in which medicines and therapies are customized to specific physiological and even DNA characteristics of patients.

The third major transformational element in technology is *nanotechnology*, which currently stands at the threshold of moving from scientific discovery into widespread practical implementation. Massive efforts to devise new ways of manipulate the nanoenvironment around us are shattering the already staggering achievements in microelectrical mechanical machines. On the horizon are advances in a number of areas, including activators, actuators, and sensors.

The implications of the convergence of these various areas of rapid technological innovation are poorly understood but nevertheless critically important. The linkages are obvious. Advances in biotechnology are enabled by significantly higher levels of computation. The relentless increases in computational capability is being strengthened by the development of molecular computing. Each day, it seems, some new point of convergences surfaces. A concrete example is the Genographic Project, a five-year effort launched by the National Geographic Society, IBM, geneticist Spencer Wells, and the Waitt Family Foundation to "map" humanity's genetic journey through the ages with ten research stations across the planet.[16]

Leadership, as tested as it already is, will be stretched even further by these kinds of technological breakthroughs. Leaders will need to rapidly develop a sufficient understanding of these complex phenomena to make decisions about regulation. Such decisions will run the gamut—from ownership of information, stem cell research to human cloning, and use of nanotechnologies. Beyond that, they will need to think about a range of overarching issues, such as the impact of these technologies on privacy. Finally, stratification of access and the benefits of such technologies across countries and social segments will also be a major consideration for leaders. The gaps could become even wider than they are now.

INFORMATION AND KNOWLEDGE FLOWS

The massive growth in data, information, and knowledge flows encircling our planet represents another massive dynamic for change. We are now more nearly connected, real-time, with breaking events across the world. In the future, the information links will be all the more significant.

The production and dissemination of new data and new knowledge have profound implications for us all. They suggest both the growing perishability of knowledge and the massive challenge for all of us to stay current in our chosen field. Furthermore, the level of global connectedness enabled by advances in and expansion of information technology have brought us to the points of what Thomas Friedman characterizes as the "B student in Bethesda versus the genius in Bangalore" syndrome.[17] In times past, notes Friedman, average students in information-rich environments had much better prospects than even the very brightest students in the developing world. In today's information environment, marked by the ensuing revolution in connectivity, the situation is reversed. The "genius in Bangalore," linked with the rest of the world, is now in a far better situation.

Progressively, we will reach the stage when it becomes fully possible for us to choose the information and knowledge "truth" we want to receive. With the proliferation of information sources across the world, without ever more robust filters to establish the veracity of information and rate the quality of opinion, the potential is for a drift into knowledge and information relativism in which no single source is any more authoritative than the next. Here, I believe that academia has an especially important function to fill. It can referee the massive flows of information such that we can judge the "truth" more effectively.

No matter what the form of political governance they may have, countries across the planet will be embattled by the continued expansion of these information flows. They will serve to atomize authority structures, disperse traditional areas of consensus and consensus-making, and reduce the basis of legitimacy on which many political systems now depend. Nonstate actors will have the capacity to influence decisions as never before. Through these growing knowledge networks, groups and even individuals can mount campaigns with worldwide implications.

ECONOMIC INTEGRATION

That the increase in cross-border factor movement has been more pronounced than underlying aggregate output growth over recent decades is well established. The story of globalization, as ambiguous an expression as it is, is still unfolding, however. The speeds and volumes associated with cross-border movements are growing by the day, but that is only a part of the overall story. As we look to the future, we need to take into account fundamental and significant shifts in the balance and structure of production.

The *Economist* magazine recently carried out a historical revaluation of the global economic balance between the developed and developing worlds by readjusting historical data on the basis of purchasing power parity.[18] It yielded some important and surprising insights. Revalued, the percentage of global economic production generated by what we now call the developed world had gone from a minority share in the early 1800s to a majority share in the 1900s and has since begun to taper off. The developing world's percentage, the mirror inverse, reflects the critical increase that ensued from the period since the 1990s, when many developing countries abandoned noneconomic statist and command policies that previously had held back development. The main takeaway from the *Economist*'s reassessment is that the developed and developing worlds now stand at a 50-50 balance in global production. As we look to the future, we can expect the developing world's share to grow even more rapidly.

Why? A combination of factors will not only drive continued globalization but also accelerate the process beyond its current levels. The first of the drivers in our ever-more-wired world is the introduction of large populations to systems that are more nearly market-oriented. China and India are the key examples, but the transitions, episodic as they have been, in Russia and Brazil are also critical. Together, these four countries—the so-called "BRIC" states—could precipitate a tectonic shift in the global structure of economic production. An early forecast by a leading financial institution suggested that these four economies alone, if they can maintain their current levels of economic dynamism, could generate combined output equivalent to the G-6 countries (United States, Japan, Germany, France, United Kingdom, and France) by the year 2025. In addition, if they could maintain high levels of growth for the longer term, out to the year 2040, they could surpass the G-6 states altogether.[19] The bottom line is that a huge chunk of humanity is coming online in the global economy, and the potential consequences— both positive and negative—are only partially understood.

Another key element underlying accelerating globalization is technology. All the current debate over the phenomenon we call "outsourcing" is enabled by remarkable advances in information technology, and we can reliably anticipate that continued innovations in technology and continued diffusion of new technologies across the world will propel the integration process at even more rapid rates.

Finally, the continued growth of global companies will be a significant catalyst in the integration process. For decades, multinational corporations have played a critical role in integration by generating cross-border flows of goods, services, labor, capital, and other economic factors. On the basis of technological advances, multinationals are now in a position to integrate production processes as never before. Milton Friedman has observed that "It is possible to produce a product anywhere, using resources from anywhere, by a company located anywhere, to be sold anywhere."[20]

Both these factors suggest that global output could continue to grow considerably in the years ahead. In a far-reaching report issued last year, the National Intelligence Council projected the possibility that between the years 2000 and 2020, the global economy could expand by some 80 percent, by 50 percent in average per capita income terms.[21] That is certainly a welcome development, the continued expansion of global output in ways that generate more positive social effects, but there are a number of reasons why we should temper our enthusiasm about "next boom"-type thinking. The first is the volatility implicit in a number of key factor inputs, not least of which is energy. Second, we have witnessed a string of significant financial crises at the national (and regional) levels over recent years, and the prospect of similar dislocations in the future cannot be discounted. Third, the historically significant shift to market economies may be in some jeopardy. In Latin America, for example, we have seen a rejection of Washington-consensus reform by some of the countries that were first-movers in the renunciation of statist economics. Venezuela stands out as an example of a country in which leaders could not maintain legitimacy for reform with their own populations and ultimately became subject to populist (and antireform) forces. That country might be a precursor for other such failures to codify the benefits of economic liberalization.

Basic economic development challenges will remain. In all likelihood, a whole world will continue to be left out of the integrating global economy. The truth is that we now live in a world in which 2.8 billion people are living on less than two dollars each day, and 1.2 billion who are attempting to survive on only one dollar a day. These broader stratification issues will surface again and again—in the context of crises in governance, the exploitation by asymmetric groups of failed states, and, finally, the tremendous human costs that afflict these populations.

As we navigate through the Doha Development Round at the World Trade Organization, the important trade-offs under discussion reflect competition between the developed countries, between developed and developing world, and between the developing countries themselves. The stakes are tremendous—not only for continued economic liberalization but also for stability and security.

CONFLICT

The day September 11, 2001 drove home the painful realization that the most powerful country in the world, the country with the most powerful military, the country with the largest economy, the "hyperpower" of the international system, was vulnerable at home. Those attacks drove home the fact that in the future, the challenge to militaries will be tremendously more complicated than they were during the superpower period. With the 9/11 attacks, modern militaries were served notice that they must continue to address traditional roles and missions while at the same time they must respond to a number of new and unfamiliar threats—nonproliferation, operations to find weapons of mass destruction, peacemaking, peacekeeping, postconflict reconstruction, and a variety of other functions for which traditional militaries are not well positioned to address.

As we look to the future, the preeminent concern is that asymmetric groups will acquire and then use weapons of mass destruction (WMD). Although the savage terrorist attacks that have transpired after September 11, 2001 have been conventional in nature (i.e., Madrid and London), there can be no room for complacency with respect to the stated intentions of terrorist groups to gain access to such weapons. To contemplate the future without preparing for the possibility of WMD attacks and events is tantamount to disarming.

The new threat calculus that we must face is a combination of traditional challenges and new threats inspired by technological innovation and information movement. The top layer of threat continues to involve nuclear, but the traditional danger of a US–Soviet nuclear confrontation has been superseded by a world in which sources of nuclear weapons and materials are no longer secure and a constellation of actors—from rogue states to asymmetric groups to, possibly, individuals—are seeking to possess such capabilities. For this reason, the challenge is for us to prepare for a host of nuclear and radiological (dispersal of nuclear material through kinetic explosion) contingencies. Another critical layer of threat includes contingencies involving biological and chemical weapons. The anthrax and subsequent ricin attacks have underlined the severity of these kinds of actions, but the reality is that an enhanced pathogen could have much more far-reaching and lethal consequences. Another important layer of danger is in the information domain. The number of information-warfare countries—countries with offensive information warfare programs—has grown considerably. Beyond that, the potential use of cyber-disruption by asymmetric groups must necessarily be a major concern to national security planners. The bottom line is that a new threat calculus requires approaches above and beyond traditional responses.

The spectrum of potential enemies and adversaries has also broadened considerably. In days gone by, the major threats to our security were large militaries with equally significant orders of battle. No longer. The 1995 attack on the Alfred Murrah federal building in Oklahoma City by Timothy McVeigh ushered in a period in which nation-states no longer have a monopoly on the capacity to inflict super-violence. Progressively, groups and even individuals have access to knowledge through the Internet and other sources on how to assemble rudimentary nuclear weapons, the genetic codes of pathogens, and a range of other pieces of information that could enable them to carry out acts of large-scale violence. The 1995 sarin gas attacks on the Tokyo subway by the Aum Shinrikyo group served notice that a wide spectrum of groups are working to acquire these capabilities.

When we survey the nature of international conflicts, it quickly becomes apparent that the number of interstate conflicts is in decline while the number of intrastate conflicts is rising. The trend, to the extent it will stretch into the future, suggests the need for modern militaries to address the complexities of failed or failing states, fragile states, and dealing with weak governance structures that are inherently susceptible to internal conflicts—ethnic, religious, and so on. Such a challenge implies more integrated thinking about how to preempt such circumstances in the first place, how to reduce the intensity of conflict once it does erupt, and how to bring societies to a state of sufficient stability and security such that they do not become launching points for international movements.

THE CHALLENGE OF GOVERNANCE

How can, and should, we respond to these big global challenges? The irony is that in the face of these areas of profound change, our capacity to organize for the future is lagging behind seriously. The obstacles are well understood. Generally speaking, our organizations suffer from many of the constraints that apply to us as individuals—short-termism, compartmentalization, stove-piping, segmentation, rigidities, legacy constraints, and a conspicuous absence of overarching vision. Who can defend, for example, the structure of the U.N. Security Council in the light of the geopolitical realities today, let alone those we can anticipate in the future? Who can explain how the Department of Homeland Security is integrating all its various operations in light of the dramatically changed security outlook at home? Who understands the extent to which the private sector has strengthened its corporate governance practices in the aftermath of the Enron fiasco? And how successfully are nonprofit groups and educational institutions adapting themselves to deal with a transformed environment? These kinds of questions are emblematic of a more general predicament facing us across layers of social organization (i.e., government, private sector, civil society, and academia): How can we continually renew organizations such that we can point them toward the future?

In my view, organizations across the board are embattled by these forces of change. For their part, governments are struggling with the redefinition of many traditionally sovereign prerogatives in light of the continued growth of the private sector and most especially in light of the abrupt expansion of nongovernmental organizations (NGOs) across the world.[22] The collapse of the "dot-com" phenomenon and the collapse of Enron sent profound shockwaves through corporate governance structures across the planet and through businesses big and small. The "dot-org" world, the world of non-profit groups and NGOs, is experiencing unprecedented strains as a result of collisions of culture (i.e., volunteerism versus corporatism) and uncertainties about longer-range leadership. Even universities, which in today's world should have more conceptual and organizational flexibility than most other institutions, are often hamstrung by shorter-term priorities and constraints.

If they fail to account for longer-range trends, organizations more generally will simply continue to be overtaken by events. They will find themselves the victims of a new iteration of the "creative destruction" that Joseph Schumpeter heralded more than 60 years ago.[23] They will run the risk of becoming remnants of a time long past, with ever less applicability to the environment around them.

An important lens through which to consider these dynamics is uneven capacity of these layers of social organization to respond. As the foregoing global drivers of change continue to express themselves in the future, the difference in the capacity of government, the private sector, NGOs, academia, and other groups to respond will likely become all the more apparent. The operative question is which one of these layers of social organization will be able to respond the most rapidly—and effectively—to the change around it. The general view I have encountered is that the private sector—by far—has the capacity to adapt the most effectively. Even government officials themselves concede that more often than not, government lags in its capacity to respond. In addition, there is the issue of legitimacy and trust. In this regard, an international poll done by Gallup in 2004 for Transparency International revealed that citizens across the world regard political and law enforcement systems and the private sector as seriously corrupt.[24] Political parties, parliaments and legislatures, legal and judiciary systems, police, and the private sector were all on the top of the list as those organizations regarded as being most corrupt.

As we contemplate our ability to address future challenges, then, it becomes increasingly clear that it will be necessary for groups to cooperate across layers of social organization—across government, business, civil society, and academia. No single layer can respond fully. This kind of cooperation, however, implies the reconciliation of fundamentally different objectives, modes of operation, and—above all, perhaps—cultures. From my standpoint, it will imply ever more significant innovation in bringing together groups in strategic coalitions contoured for the specific challenges they face. Although it has encountered a number of serious difficulties, the model of the Global Fund on HIV/AIDS, Malaria and Tuberculosis may be instructive.[25] It consists of an international organizational platform with sovereign state participation as well as the involvement of the private sector and NGOs.

A precursor to progress is strategic leadership. Leaders across disciplines will need to be far-sighted, creative, and show the capacity to implement their ideas of how to effect reform. Against the wave of short-termism we face, they are in ever shorter supply.

IMPLICATIONS FOR ETHICAL LEADERSHIP

When taken together, the change that we can envisage in these seven areas suggests the need for far-sighted leadership animated by vision and innovative approaches. This, I believe, is where the mandate of institutions of higher education is especially important. Our overarching challenge is to provide the knowledge for leaders to develop vision, to inculcate them with the understanding to execute on their vision, and to help them develop a conceptual and ethical foundation on which difficult—sometimes, excruciating—trade-offs will have to be made.

This suggests a fundamental reassessment of the sources of strategic leadership, not only in the United States but also across the world and not only in government but also across disciplines. Such a reassessment would ask how we develop our leaders, how we condition their thinking, what their moral and ethical frameworks are, and what priorities for action are being contemplated. I believe that our institutions of higher education, again, should be the platform for such a reappraisal.

I worry that we are experiencing a steady and relentless erosion in our capability to exercise such strategic leadership. Leadership is being replaced by management, strategy by tactics, long-term planning by triage reactions, principle by expediency, and far-sighted vision by mere management by the numbers. If we are to respond to the longer-range challenges that loom in front of us, it means that new paradigms, new approaches, and new and authentically strategic leadership will be necessary.

In light of the foregoing, Mahatma Gandhi's observation that "[y]ou must be the change you want to see in the world" assumes new and more urgent meaning. The essence of ethical leadership in the 21st century, in the face of these challenges, will demand a broader vision, new approaches to action, and the capacity to shatter the culture of short-termism enveloping us all.

CHAPTER 2

The Three Elements of Good Leadership in Rapidly Changing Times

Lynn Barendsen and Howard Gardner

What does it mean to be a "good" leader? What are the traits of good leaders across time and how do these leaders adjust to rapidly changing times? Over the past decade, we and our fellow researchers on the GoodWork® Project have interviewed over 1200 individuals in a variety of professions, at different levels in their careers[1] (see also http://www.goodworkproject.org). Our research suggests that the best leaders are individuals who, in their work, exhibit three distinct meanings of good: (1) an Excellent technical and professional quality and competence; (2) an Ethical orientation; and (3) a completely Engaged sense of fulfillment and meaningfulness. We think of these as three "E's" intertwined in the DNA of our best leaders, of whom Betty Siegel is certainly one.

Good leadership is never easy or unproblematic. Few Ages appear "golden" to those who are living through them. Yet leadership is especially challenged when new technologies are rampant, when markets are very powerful, and when few if any forces can counteract them. Certainly our Age is a paradigm of such conditions. That said, one can always learn from leaders who coped with such uncertain conditions without losing their sense of purpose.

One example of such a leader is the late John Gardner, no relation to either author, and, as it happens, an expert on the subject of leadership. Gardner served six different U.S. Presidents. Among his many other accomplishments, he was Secretary of Health, Education and Welfare, Founder of Common Cause, Founder of the National Urban Coalition, and President of the Carnegie Corporation. He authored numerous books during his lifetime, including *Excellence*, *Self-Renewal*, and *On Leadership*.

As part of our study we interviewed John Gardner in 1999 and again in 2000. (We also dedicated our 2001 book, *Good Work*, to him[1].) Gardner sought excellence in every domain—he memorably observed that excellence in plumbing was as important as excellence in philosophy. But excellence was not a single level, to be reached and maintained; rather, in his view, excellence must be continually renewed. Reaching a high level of success or meeting high personal standards can actually harbor risks:

> I had already written the book on *Excellence* or I was toward having written it, and becoming aware of this other dimension of vitality and stagnation, and I went to an institution, which again I won't name, but it was of unquestioned quality, and yet some things in it were just foreboding of stagnation. I mean that if they *didn't* mend it, they were going to be dead in the water. And I thought, gee, excellence isn't enough. And a curious thing about some of these great, highly developed fields is that they can be on the edge of stagnation and still so good that you can't help admire them. But they're weaving their shroud. They are not building for the future.[2]

In his own career, Gardner certainly did not stagnate. He continually evolved, from professor to foundation president to high-level official to social reformer, actively pursuing change as soon as he started to feel too comfortable in any one setting. Gardner pushed himself to move beyond his current level of excellence. In our study, we have confirmed that sustaining excellent and ethical work is difficult, once meaningful engagement begins to fray. As he told us:

> . . . I began to think about renewal while I was at Carnegie, and I wrote the book while I was at Carnegie, and it was really the principle of renewal plus the confidence I had that led me to take the government job. For a good year before I was offered the job, I had real feelings that my situation was too comfortable. I knew all the answers to being a foundation president in New York City. I was able to open practically any door and deal with my problems, and that's not a good sign. I mean, you know that life isn't like that, so if you begin to feel that way, something's closing in on you.[3]

To paraphrase Gardner, once success has been achieved, work may cease to be engaging.

As we construe it, ethical work is socially responsible work, work that takes its consequences into account and adjusts accordingly. Asked about leadership, Gardner responded in ethical terms. In his view, leadership goes hand-in-hand with thinking beyond oneself:

> . . . I began to think about "How do you develop leaders?" And it clearly traces back to childhood and early development of a sense of responsibility for the other. And you can't lead if you don't give a damn about the other. Leaders are people who are thinking, even if they are not thinking in kindly or beneficial ways, they are thinking about other people. They are relating themselves to the group. When I began to work on community building, same thing. You go back to people's early involvement with the group and their relation to it. And a lot of the breakdowns in individual performance that lead to delinquency and so forth and so on are people who never learned, never developed any bond with the group. No feedback from the group to govern the individual's behavior because they discounted that.[4]

In Gardner's view, ethical work, without excellence, is equally ineffective. For example, he describes "bad" non-profits, mismanaged organizations that stumble along, trying to do good and yet lacking innovation and expertise. These nonprofits are "bad,"

> . . . bad in the sense of pious continuance of not competent or creative work, which in a way is damaging. Damaging because it uses up well meaning dollars, because it breeds discouragement in people who just feel "We're working so hard and we're just not getting anywhere." And I think there's a fair amount of that in the nonprofit world. And there's something about lofty ideals that are at odds with clean-cut self-evaluation. You know, "How can you criticize us when our ideals are so great?" That's why I like that cartoon of Peanuts on the pitcher's mound saying, "How can we lose when we're so sincere?"[5]

John Gardner helps us to contextualize the three "E's" of good leadership. Leadership without excellence, even well-intentioned leadership, results in mediocrity. Leadership without ethics is encountered in every sphere, from politics to business to the nonprofit world. Leadership without engagement simply cannot be sustained, and eventually results in burnout or in compromised work.

CURRENT CONDITIONS THAT COMPLEXIFY THE TASK OF LEADERSHIP

Strong counterforces threaten excellence, ethics, and engagement. Indeed, in an era of rapid change, even the identification of that which is good can be difficult. These powerful forces must either be controlled or they will control us. In what follows, we comment on three conditions that challenge efforts to achieve good work: the forces of globalization, the struggle to raise funds in a market-saturated milieu, and the scarcity of positive examples of leadership.

Globalization

Over the last few decades, we have come to recognize forces that constitute globalization. In this era, all manner of entities—currencies, customs, commodities, communicable diseases, to name a few—circulate around the world with enormous speed, and without regard to boundaries and borders of any sort. Events that occur in areas as remote as North Korea, Afghanistan, or Silicon Valley exert almost immediate effects on populations thousands of miles away. Because many of these factors are difficult to understand, let alone to control, it is easy to lose one's ethical bearings—and thus sacrifice the chance to do good work.

Jill Ker Conway, teacher, author, feminist historian, served as President of Smith College for ten years. For his book, *Shared Values for a Troubled World*, our colleague. Rushworth Kidder interviewed Conway. During the interview at her home in a Boston suburb, Conway describes one of the problems associated with globalization:

> I just came back from a board meeting of a major international service company . . . Everybody knows the world is one world: they trade twenty-four hours a day in many different currencies, and you would not have to persuade anybody there that we live in a single global environment. But when I go out to dinner in a suburb like this, it is not apparent to people at all.[6]

Although globalization is an indisputable fact, the multifaceted ways in which it affects every one of us are not always obvious. And therefore, motivating individuals to acknowledge and act while keeping global conditions in mind is challenging. Conway describes a world "so complex and complicated that it is impossible to imagine any oversight (i.e. careful supervision— Ed. note) by professionals."[7] When asked about a solution to these issues, Conway points directly to ethical leadership, "young ones learn their ethics from the adult generation. So we have to model a greater ethical concern."[8]

William Drayton is the founder of Ashoka, one of the very first organizations designed to fund social entrepreneurs (individuals who approach social problems with entrepreneurial spirit and business sense). Ashoka seeks out leaders who will tackle social issues of global consequence. Most of the Fellows come from and serve the third world, including many countries that fail to thrive in the global economy. To be selected as an Ashoka fellow, applicants go through an intensive screening process. Drayton emphasizes the ethical component to this evaluation:

> One of our four criteria is ethical fiber for selecting fellows, and ditto for staff. It's not accidental, it's very carefully thought through, as we think that values are absolutely critical. They're critical for efficacy. You can't get people to change the primary patterns in what they do in their lives, which involves all sorts of subtle power changes, unless they trust you. You can't lead people if they don't trust you. And I don't believe that you can fake it . . . We can't build a fellowship, which absolutely requires openness and trust and mutual respect, if even a tiny number of people were not trustworthy . . . we just don't want to add to [the] supply of untrustworthy public figures.[9]

According to Drayton, finding and funding these new leaders will accelerate the process of positive social change:

> We want people who have society's interests at heart. That's why we are here. We're not a social welfare program for bright people . . . We're trying to have – to speed up the rate of change and democratization in the world. And these folks just happen to be the single most critical component to that change.[10]

Drayton is one of many leaders determined to use globalization to positive effect. Ashoka seeks out social entrepreneurs who have developed solutions that may be replicated worldwide. Here, "ethical fiber" is described as one element that is used not so much to *combat* globalization but rather to turn the fact of our smaller, faster world into positive results.

At its worst, globalization may be seen as a threat (how do we ever create positive connections and resonances in such a diverse, and nonegalitarian world?). At its best, globalization may be seen as an invitation to embrace diversity. Cellist Yo-Yo Ma has done exactly this with his Silk Road Project. Born in 1955 to Chinese parents, Ma began studying the cello at the age of four. His parents soon moved to New York City, where he began studying at the Julliard School. After Julliard, he attended Harvard College, and since his graduation, he has performed with many of the world's leading orchestras. He has won fifteen Grammy Awards, recorded over fifty albums, and in addition to his expertise with classical music, he is well-versed in contemporary and folk music.

The Silk Road Project is in part an expansion of these varied musical interests. Founded in 1998, this project examines the global movement of music and ideas and explores ways in which our current cultural understanding might be enhanced by traditional expressions. As Ma explains:

> We live in a world of increasing awareness and interdependence, and I believe that music can act as a magnet to draw people together. Music is an expressive

art that can reach to the very core of one's identity. By listening to and learning from the voices of an authentic musical tradition, we become increasingly able to advocate for the worlds they represent. Further, as we interact with unfamiliar musical traditions we encounter voices that are not exclusive to one community. We discover transnational voices that belong to one world.[11]

Complementing Conway's and Drayton's emphasis on the ethical dimensions, Ma helps us to understand that excellence and engagement are also crucial to this formula. First, he describes how bringing together some of the world's best musicians is crucial to the creative process:

> We seem to have two main jobs—to investigate and give credit to the past, on the one hand, and then to encourage new kinds of cultural development, on the other. All cultures evolve. And since we're more and more connected in this global world, we can't say, well, we'll keep something separate. That is certainly one way to kill cultural expressions very quickly . . . I think this is a moment in time when it's appropriate to bring specialists together to see whether we can find a consensus about common knowledge that will enrich our own specialties.[12]

Reminiscent of the process of renewal described (and lived) by Gardner, this type of work involves an openness to learning that confers new meaning upon work. Very much like John Gardner, Yo-Yo Ma has broadened his classical musical repertoire to include all kinds of contemporary music; and he has participated in a number of collaborative innovations, including a six-part multimedium television series. As a result of this continuing artistic stretch, Ma remains fully engaged:

> For me, one of the things that stimulates both scholarship and creativity is new knowledge. In this (Silk Road) project we're on a steep learning curve because we're constantly faced with the unfamiliar—whether different cultures, languages, musical instruments or disciplines. All that I'm learning will certainly change the way I play the cello, and it will change the way I think about the world.[13]

One solution, then, to the challenge globalization poses to leadership, is to embrace it, to see it as a strength rather than as an obstacle. Muhammad Yunus, professor of economics in Bangladesh and social entrepreneur par excellence, started the Grameen Bank—an institution that pioneered micro-credit lending (providing very small loans to individuals with little or no credit history). Like others in the "subspecies" of human social entrepreneur,

Yunus often sees possibility where others see complication. His perspective envisions the empowerment of underserved populations—with globalization as a great equalizer:

> Borders will be relics of the past ... The closeness will come ... What you've got in Washington, I'll have in a tiny township with a population of 403-because I've got access to information. So you're not so big any more. You can't come and tell me, 'You don't know what's going on in tiny countries; you have to be in Washington to find out.' I say, 'You're crazy: I know everything!'[14]

Market Pressures

Especially for those whose vocation is explicitly the pursuit of good work, obtaining sufficient funding is a perpetual problem. Most such individuals work for nonprofit institutions, like hospitals or universities, or for the over one million nongovernmental organizations that have sprung up in the last half century. The issue of survival is exacerbated today because nonprofit organizations are expected to follow business models—to have business plans, to produce 'deliverables', to be accountable in terms of numbers of pregnancies prevented, new audience members secured, or engineers graduated—even when such quantitative measures are inappropriate, given the mission and mode of operation of nonprofit organizations. Monetary pressures cross professional boundaries—everyone has a bottom line to which he or she is held accountable.

Derek Bok, the former President of Harvard University, has written extensively on this topic in *Universities in the Marketplace*. The influences acting upon the university, making it an increasingly commercial venture, are numerous:

> ... commercialization turns out to have multiple causes. Financial cutbacks undoubtedly acted as a spur to profit-seeking for some universities and some departments. The spirit of private enterprise and entrepreneurship that became so prominent in the 1980s helped encourage and legitimate such initiatives. A lack of clarity about academic values opened the door even wider. Keener competition gave still further impetus. But none of these stimuli would have borne such abundant fruit had it not been for the rapid growth of money-making opportunities provided by a more technologically sophisticated, knowledge-based economy.[15]

New leaders—and in particular, innovative leaders, those who are busy trying to establish new models for change—need a specific type of support. Drayton describes the issue as follows:

> Entrepreneurs need loyalty. They need partners who will understand that they have got to go through, that *they (the entrepreneurs)* are the golden goose. You don't need this if you're putting in the fifteenth department store or another school . . . But you do when you're fundamentally changing the pattern, because that entrepreneurial mindset is constantly going after every little change. And it's changing the idea. They're evolving it. If you don't invest in the entrepreneur, forget it. It's going to fail. Most foundations and governments have very little sense of who the entrepreneur is or why they've got to invest for ten years in the entrepreneur and help him or her through this long cycle. The time frame is also completely wrong. And the entrepreneur needs a large sum of money, not little dribs and drabs . . . There is a complete misfit between what the entrepreneur needs and what these institutions provide.[16]

When new leaders are forced to spend an inordinate amount of time seeking funding, their work frequently suffers. Time spent fundraising necessitates time away from work, and quality of work may suffer as a result. Sometimes, funding pressures can result in less-than-honest practices—what we term "compromised work". Some individuals may spin the truth to make projects more attractive to potential funders, while others may take more drastic measures. In our study of young professionals, in particular, we often heard the justification of improper (if not frankly illegal) means in service of noble ends or long-term goals. (The theory: Once power and position have been achieved, one will miraculously be transferred into a paragon of virtue[17].) Market forces, such as funding pressures, constitute a perennial challenge to today's leaders.

One solution, especially apt for entrepreneurial leaders, is to provide long-term funding. In the past few years, this support has become possible, due to the emergence of venture philanthropy. Often entrepreneurs themselves, venture philanthropists understand the mindset and the needs of these creative leaders and are therefore more inclined and more able to give them the long-term support they require. As one venture philanthropist describes it, the funding process really becomes a collaborative relationship:

> . . . engaged philanthropy relies on collaboration and real shared decision making . . . It depends a lot on trust, and trust takes time, so we make long-term investments that allow for the engagement to grow organically over the

time that we're working with a particular group. I don't think you can do engaged philanthropy well if you just make a one-time grant.[18]

Such general, long-term support can indeed free entrepreneurial leaders to carry out good work. But this happy ending can only come about if the venture philanthropist respects the operation of the nonprofit and does not attempt to micromanage the organization or distort its mission. It is great for venture philanthropists to become engaged; but it is risky if this engagement threatens the excellence or the ethics of the funded organization.

Other approaches are conceivable. To resist commercialization in higher education, Derek Bok advocates a systemic change:

> Others may think of further steps to help university leaders resist the excesses of commercialization. Whatever the precise reforms, however, the basic point remains: success demands much more than simply announcing an appropriate set of rules. Unless universities create an environment in which the prevailing incentives and procedures reinforce intellectual standards instead of weakening them, commercial temptations are bound to take a continuing toll on essential academic values.[19]

As president of a well-regarded university, Bok set very high standards for the leaders of our institutions of higher learning—standards of ethics and excellence. This example is particularly important because tomorrow's leaders are being molded within these institutions. Here they will witness and learn a great deal about leadership—of varying qualities and quality.

Scarcity of Positive Examples

Leadership can also be threatened by a dearth of positive models. In a very basic sense, young people learn by example. When the individuals who are garnering public attention are successful by dint of dishonest means, or in the news because their corrupt actions have been pardoned, many young people are likely to follow suit. And when the flaws of even the most impressive leaders are sensationalized in the media, future leaders may come to believe that good work—excellent, ethical, engaging work—is impossible.

As a long-time leader in the field of education, Bok has garnered much admiration for his attention to ethical issues and the very impressive standards embodied by him and his wife, the philosopher Sissela Bok. In his interview with Rushworth Kidder, Bok makes an explicit connection between ethics and leadership. Referring to major social concerns (poverty, crime, welfare, public education), Bok argues that solutions to these issues must go beyond changes in policy and beyond acquisition of knowledge. Change must begin with the ethical qualities of our leaders, many of whom frequent our university settings:

> . . . efforts to respond to the kinds of public problems that I'm talking about cannot be sought only in developing the knowledge for policy solutions . . . [also needed is] a strengthening of individual virtues, ethical virtues, civic virtues on the part of individuals—especially the kinds of influential individuals who flow through our colleges and universities.[20]

Clearly, if they are to catalyze good work, leaders need ethics as well as knowledge, information, and IQ points.

It is important to acknowledge that leaders and leadership are rarely properly located in a single, authoritative individual. In his conversation with Kidder, John Gardner says "I think of leaders as running down through all levels and segments of the system.[21]" He cites problems with leadership in the United States, in part, because of a breakdown in this system of leadership, "we need a much healthier substratum of leaders down the line before we can get great leadership at the top.[22]" Such a substratum is most unlikely to arise in the absence of role models that are convincing and worthy of emulation.

It is possible that practical interventions in our schools may encourage the development of ethical, excellent, and engaged leaders. (One of us [Howard Gardner] has in recent years collaborated with Betty Siegel in an international effort at the collegiate level.) At our GoodWork® Project, we have developed one such intervention, a GoodWork® Toolkit.[23] This instrument provides a framework for individuals to consider the kind of workers they are now and the kinds of professionals they want to become. Designed originally for high school students, it has been piloted in middle schools, high schools, and university settings, and has been used as a professional development tool. This Toolkit encourages excellent and meaningful work while at the same time evoking reflections about the consequences of one's work on others.

It is important to stress that exemplary leaders do exist. Because of the pathographical bias of current media, they are simply not garnering considerable attention. (Magazines devoted to the presentation of good work do not survive, while many of those that focus on the foibles of the great and the not-so-great sell in the millions.) John Gardner spoke to this issue:

> . . . you've probably heard me talk about the number of Jefferson's and Washington's and the like around today. Six world-class leaders when we had a population of three million. We now have eighty times that many, we ought to have eighty times six—four hundred and eighty Jefferson's, Madison's,

Franklin's, Washington's. And I'm convinced they're out there. I don't throw up my hands and say, "Where are they?" They're out there, not fully aware of their capacity to lead because it isn't a big crisis. Not conscious of what they have to give the world.[24]

If Gardner is correct in his belief, another solution would be to find and inspire these potential leaders. Preferably, this can happen before the crisis Gardner alludes to, one that makes our need for leadership even more apparent.

Up to this point we have cited leaders who are personally known to us, but numerous other exemplary models could be mentioned. To cite a particularly vivid example, Anita Roddick, founder of the Body Shop chain of stores, continually examines her work and her values, and does so *keeping in mind that she is an example* to young people:

I . . . travel with the vagabond for two or three weeks, just going through the black belt of America. Living in shacks. Seeing crack . . . being made, living outside, in prison communities. It is incredibly important that I continue to do that, whether it's [the] Appalachian trip or whether it's the Albanian trip. It's so important because that's a role of leadership. A leader in my eyes is not someone who sits of top of an ivory tower, lots of dosh, lots of money, and proclaims it. It is moral leadership. It's doing things that the young girls or young people that work with me can say, "God she did that. Now what does that make me?" And how do I—my job is, how do you keep them away from a value system of endless increasing wealth to one where humanity, community, is part of the value system.[25]

Roddick holds her business accountable to high standards of both excellence and ethics. At the time of our interview (in 1999), she struck us as fully engaged with her network of enterprises. Asked how she balances work with family, she replied, "I don't. One bloody big creative stew. Because what is work to me isn't work." Roddick has achieved a fair amount of attention in the media. However, our study on Good Work confirms that there are many other exemplary leaders—or potential exemplary leaders—who are either unnoticed or are unaware of their abilities to lead.

CONCLUSION

Threats to effective leadership today are very real, as real as the power of markets, the dystopic flavor of the press, and the rapid and unpredictable emergence of new technologies. Prescient leaders have already discerned methods to transform these threats into opportunities. Yo-Yo Ma does not worry about globalization, but instead, shows us how it can diversify and deepen our cultural understandings. He does so as one of the world's premier cellists, fully engaged in his music, and equally engaged in his service of others. William Drayton, frustrated by the lack of funding for the socially minded leaders of the future, founded an organization designed to alleviate the problem. He has become a leader amongst social entrepreneurs, a group that by definition acts with innovation and on behalf of others, and a group that is almost universally engaged in meaningful work. As a result of her business success, Anita Roddick found herself in a position of power. She used her position self-consciously, to model the behavior of a good leader, trying to combat less positive examples. It is as important to know of these exemplary three workers—and of the individual, Betty Siegel, being honored in these pages—as it is to know about the sins and peccadilloes of Arthur Andersen, Enron, Martha Stewart, Dennis Kozlowski, Courtney Love, or Michael Jackson. The individuals portrayed here illustrate that good leaders are able to turn potential threats into strategies that can help others—leaders or followers—to execute good work.

ACKNOWLEDGMENTS

For support of the GoodWork Project we would like to thank The Christian Johnson Endeavor Foundation, The Hewlett Foundation, The Atlantic Philanthropies, Louise and Claude Rosenberg, and Jeffrey Epstein. For his contribution to the line of thought developed in this paper, we thank Rush Kidder of the Institute for Global Ethics.

CHAPTER 3

Leadership, Accountability, and the Deficit of Public Trust

John C. Knapp

"What if it turns out that globalization subjects all of us to faceless forces unaccountable for any of the considerable human suffering still prevalent across the world?" Such a question might be expected from a demonstrator at a meeting of the World Trade Organization. But it may surprise some that it was raised by Deval Patrick, who at the time was The Coca-Cola Company's executive vice president, general counsel and corporate secretary.

Mr. Patrick's question was somewhat rhetorical, for he was making the point that remaining faceless and unaccountable is simply not an option for leaders of global organizations. "A rising cadre of advocacy organizations—themselves global in scope, informed, organized and politically savvy—compels us to pay more attention to social concerns," he said, adding:

> For businesses trying to succeed globally it is becoming harder to avert our eyes from people crushed by poverty or human rights abuses. Or to diminish the significance of the predictable human errors or oversights that arise in the running of any business.
>
> We cannot avert our eyes because the media won't let us. The Internet won't let us. Our own people in the field won't let us. In an ironic way, globalization itself won't let us.[1]

We live in a time when many of the old assumptions about leadership no longer seem to apply. Leaders are confronted by demands for accountability never before imagined, even as they face a global society that has been described as distrustful, unforgiving, and deeply cynical. Few are fully up to the task.

THE TRUST DEFICIT

By nearly every measure, public trust of institutions and their leaders—from government to business to social services—has been in decline for at least two decades. And the trend is accelerating in the new century, giving rise to unprecedented challenges for even the best leaders. Where once they may have assumed followers and other stakeholders trusted them unless some circumstance caused a loss of confidence, today's leaders are wise to treat trust as an elusive asset that is difficult to build and easy to lose. Far from taking trust for granted, they must recognize that others may be less prone than ever to take them at their word or give them the benefit of the doubt.

To paraphrase Amartya Sen, the 1998 Nobel laureate in economics, trust is like oxygen: we notice only when it seems to be in short supply. It should come as no surprise, then, that a mounting body of research validates a deficit of trust that many leaders have already noticed.

World Economic Forum's 2005 global opinion survey, which involved more than 20,000 respondents in 20 countries, revealed an "alarming picture of declining levels of trust" in institutions, which had dropped precipitously since the tracking study began in January 2001.[2] While the sharpest declines involved national governments and the United Nations, trust of corporations reached it lowest mark since the study began—despite countermeasures like the 2002 Sarbanes–Oxley corporate reform legislation enacted by the U.S. Congress to restore public trust in the financial markets.

How does World Economic Forum define trust? Respondents were read a list of institutions and asked how much they trust each "to operate in the best interests of our society." To be sure, there are other ways of describing and measuring trust, but this method has particular value in gauging the extent to which institutions are perceived as serving the common good. Overall, fewer than half of those surveyed had even "some" trust in national governments, large domestic companies, news media, global companies, or trade unions.

A parallel study by the same organization, completed in 2002 found that *leaders* of institutions enjoyed even less trust than the institutions they lead. In this survey, respondents were asked a slightly different question, "How much do you trust the following leaders to manage the challenges of the coming year in the best interests of you and your family."[3] Here are some of the findings:

A connection between trust and the ethics of leaders is seen clearly in the factor deemed by respondents to be most important in establishing and maintaining trust. When asked about the attributes necessary for them

Type of Leader	Percent of Population with "A Lot" or "Some" Trust
Religious leaders	41
Leaders of Western Europe	36
Managers of global economy	36
Managers of national economy	35
Executives of multinational companies	33
Leaders of the USA	27

to trust leaders, they overwhelmingly named *honesty* (49 percent). Other important attributes were *vision* (15 percent), *experience* (12 percent), *intellect* (10 percent), and *compassion* (5 percent). Conversely, the characteristics or behaviors most damaging to trust were: *not doing what they say* (45 percent), *self-interest* (28 percent), *secrecy* (11 percent), *arrogance* (8 percent), and *character flaws* (5 percent). We conclude that there is a strong link between trust and the ethical conduct of leaders, specifically truth-telling and promise-keeping.

Research findings in the United States mirror the global decline in trust of institutions. According to a Lichtman–Zogby Interactive survey of 8,000 adults in April 2006, three out of four Americans said they trust the government less than they did five years earlier. Only 5 percent said corporations "do right by the consumers they are in business to serve," and just 3 percent thought the U.S. Congress was trustworthy.[4] Though the statistics vary, other studies yield similarly disturbing evidence of distrust of a range of institutions and leaders fundamental to society.[5]

FORCES ERODING TRUST

Despite these studies documenting the extent of the trust deficit, researchers are not in complete agreement about its root causes. There is no question, however, that widespread doubt about the ethics of leaders is a major contributing factor. Whether this perception results from an *actual* increase in misconduct (e.g., corporate malfeasance, political corruption, clergy sex scandals), or simply from heightened *awareness* of such failures is less clear, for there is some evidence that ethical failures by leaders of institutions occur no more frequently today than in decades past. Whether or not the conduct of leaders has taken a radical turn for the worse, several broader social trends certainly contribute to the erosion of trust.

Relentless News Coverage

The availability of 24-hour news via television, radio, and the Internet has given the media unprecedented influence in countries around the world. This constant stream of information about government, business, and other institutions is heavily weighted toward negative events, concerns, and allegations. Social psychologists and communication theorists have long understood the powerful role of mass media in "mediating reality" by cultivating and even constructing social meaning for individuals.[6] But unlike the days when three national television networks provided Americans a half an hour of news once a day, the presence of media in our lives is a pervasive and ever-present influence. The drumbeat of headlines chronicling the missteps of some leaders has a corrosive effect on public trust and confidence in all leaders.

Instantaneous, Limitless Information

The Internet has opened a wide, global pipeline of information about institutions and their leaders. The fact that much of it is neither reliable nor authoritative did not deter the 1 billion users[7] who went online in 2005 to search for information across billions of web pages. Consider the implications for corporate leadership, as employees no longer rely solely on their employer to learn what is happening down the hall or across the globe, but instead look to the World Wide Web and exchange e-mails with others at the new, global version of the office water cooler. Over time, many of them conclude they must trust themselves, and not their leaders, for information about things that may affect their livelihood.

Institutional and Social Change

The pace of institutional change in the developed world has reordered relationships and severed many traditional bonds of dependency and loyalty. In postmodern society, people find themselves changing jobs, homes, and affiliations with social and religious institutions with far greater frequency than previous generations. Consequently, many feel less inclined to depend on leaders of traditional institutions to look after their best interests. Trust takes time to build and is largely a product of stable relationships characterized by "consistent behavior, regular and candid communication, and a mutual commitment to achieve common goals."[8] The opportunity to build such relationships is less available to today's leaders than to their predecessors.

WHY TRUST MATTERS

No doubt many other factors are fueling the trust deficit. However, whatever the causes may be, the effects on leaders and society are being felt worldwide. At the *macrosystemic* level, we know that trust is essential to the survival of democracy and free enterprise. Robert Putnam and others show that the viability of democratic institutions rests on civic engagement and voluntary cooperation, both requiring an ample supply of trust as the social capital exchanged by citizens.[9] Likewise, commerce flourishes only when participants believe they can trust one another, limiting the need for laws to regulate every aspect of every transaction. Never was there a better illustration of this principle than when the accounting-related scandals came to light at Enron Corporation, WorldCom Corporation, Arthur Andersen, and other leading businesses in the United States. Their breaches of trust, in the form of dishonesty with shareholders and employees, undermined investor confidence and left the financial markets reeling. In the absence of voluntary, trustworthy behavior by these firms' leaders, the Congress enacted costly new regulations that many corporate executives complained were unfair to the vast majority of companies that were not part of the problem. Yet the legislative response was a recognition that a market economy cannot survive if investors do not trust the system.

At the *meso*, or organizational, level trust is the basis of all taken-for-granted aspects of relationships, providing leaders the benefit of the doubt when problems arise. It also determines receptivity to institutional and leadership communications in what Richard Smith calls the "trust-communication cycle."[10] Better yet, there is empirical evidence that trust has a measurable, positive effect on organizational performance. James Coleman contends "a group whose members manifest trustworthiness and place extensive trust in one another will be able to accomplish much more than a comparable group lacking that trustworthiness and trust."[11] Perhaps the best explanation of the value of trust in organizations comes from the research of Robert Levering who developed the criteria used to compile *Fortune*'s annual list of the "100 Best Companies to Work for in America." He writes, "Perhaps we can explain the apparent success of good workplaces in a straightforward way: Good workplaces are defined by having a high degree of trust. . . ." His Trust Index, an instrument comprising dozens of questions administered to employees, is a predictor of employee retention, morale and productivity. Trust, Levering says, is "awfully good grease"[12] that must be applied by leaders at all levels of responsibility.

This concept was validated in dramatic fashion by a study involving 6,500 employees at 76 Holiday Inn hotels in North America. Employees were asked to rank their managers' performance in following through on promises and practicing what they preach, and their responses were correlated with each hotel's data on customer satisfaction and financial performance. The conclusion: a one-eighth point improvement in a manager's "trust score" on a five-point scale translated to an annual profit increase of more than $250,000 for the individual hotel property.[13]

Other research has linked trust to positive job attitudes, organizational justice, psychological contracts, and effective conflict management.[14] The Ethics Resource Center's study of ethics in the workplace finds that U.S. employees who trust employers are significantly more likely (1) to believe management has integrity and is fair, honest, and concerned about people; (2) to be committed to ethical practices in the workplace; (3) to share ethical concerns and report misconduct to management; and (4) to conduct themselves in an ethical manner in relationships with coworkers and customers.[15]

Finally, at the *micro*, or individual leader, level it has been shown that career-ending failures are very often attributable to a loss of followers' trust.[16] As the indispensable ingredient in healthy and effective relationships, trust has two vital dimensions—intrafollower (horizontal) and leader-follower (vertical)—both of which are products of leaders' actions and reputation for competence and ethics.[17]

Yet for all that has been learned by scholars and others who study the subject, leaders know that establishing and sustaining trust today is easier said than done. "It is hard to create, very valuable and quite fragile," says Joseph Badaracco.[18] Leadership sage Max De Pree cautions that it does not accrue automatically to leaders, nor can it be "bought or commanded, inherited or enforced." Rather, it grows as a result of *"translating personal integrity into institutional fidelity*. At the heart of fidelity lies truth-telling and promise-keeping,"[19] the very same leadership attributes most valued by respondents in the World Economic Forum's global opinion survey. De Pree's philosophy is consistent with Robert Greenleaf's notion of servant leadership, which James Tatum says can be boiled down to a single word:

> I choose the word 'trust' because it connects us all in a common but important way. It is a word that describes the results of actions conforming to all of the . . . values. It brings forth an experiential meaning and an intuitive one. . . .
>
> Think of it this way. Suppose every decision is prefaced with deliberate questions: "Will this build trust?" "Will it build long-term trust?" "How might it destroy trust?" Such a simple approach is not so simple. It really means that we have an obligation to train our minds to encompass all of the values with one vision and have an ability to apply the issue of building trust with wholeness.[20]

AN ERA OF HYPERACCOUNTABILITY

Deval Patrick is right. Nothing has made 21st-century leadership more difficult than the growing chorus of voices from all quarters demanding that leaders give account publicly for their priorities, decisions, and actions. And no place is this chorus more vocal than the so-called "blogosphere," where tens of millions of Web logs (a number that is doubling every six months) are maintained by individuals, small groups, and large organizations alike, frequently for the express purpose of criticizing or questioning the actions of institutions and leaders. Bloggers provided real-time, on-the-scene reports on the Iraq war, hurricane Katrina's destruction of New Orleans, and the December 2004 tsunami that devastated parts of Southern Asia—often ahead of official statements from leaders encumbered by bureaucracies, and sometimes undermining leaders' perceived competence and credibility in the process.

Bloggers also are playing pivotal roles in events at the organization level. In 2005, news of a major corporation's acquisition by a holding company was leaked by a blogger in advance of the public announcement. During the months-long transition to new ownership, employees and investors discovered that Web logs provided more useful and up-to-date information than the corporate web site. In the same way, bloggers and online discussion forums frequently play influential, if unofficial, roles in employer–labor negotiations.

Even the news media feel the effects of bloggers, some of whom helped shorten the careers of CBS News Anchor Dan Rather and *New York Times* Executive Editor Howell Raines by posting information that proved more accurate than accounts published by the news organizations themselves. Neither are religious leaders immune to the effects of the blogosphere, described by sociologist Lorne Dawson as "the realm where anyone who has an ax to grind against a religion . . . can find hundreds of sites online."[21] Bloggers run the gamut from Mormons questioning church policy to Muslims challenging traditional views of women to Roman Catholics airing allegations of clergy sexual misconduct.

One characteristic of electronic communication, in all its forms, is the speed with which it spreads and reproduces information. As Mr. Patrick observed, it was not long ago that a global company's local problem in Asia would remain a local concern. But today the same issue can be publicized on an Asian Web log and within an hour repeated countless times by nongovernmental organizations (the number of which has grown exponentially in the first five years of the century), labor organizations, news media, and employees around the world. One news report noted, "In an era of user-generated content, companies may be losing control of what is said about them."[22]

This explosion of near-instantaneous communication is intensifying the pressure on leaders to monitor and respond to concerns voiced by sources legitimate and not so legitimate, a problem complicated by the difficulty stakeholders encounter in discerning which sources are actually reliable and authoritative. How do leaders effectively communicate and respond to information (and misinformation) in this environment? And, as they do so, how do they avoid becoming preoccupied with reading and attempting to influence the unmanageable flow of information on the information superhighway?

TOWARD EMOTIONALLY INTELLIGENT LEADERSHIP

There are no easy answers to these questions, but it is clear that refusing to engage others, including critics, willingly and openly is not only unwise, it may be suicidal. Because the global forces driving down trust are beyond the control of even the largest institutions, we need leaders suited to the new climate, leaders who understand the nature of trust and how it is built and sustained. Twenty-first–century leadership requires a renewed commitment to listening intentionally, speaking honestly, acting with integrity, and seeking outcomes that serve the best interests of all concerned.

In other words, the world needs ethical leaders with a healthy measure of what is sometimes called emotional intelligence. Emotionally intelligent leaders resonate with others through a dynamic blending of social awareness and self-awareness, which work together to establish healthy, trust-based relationships. Being socially aware means to be empathetic, "attuned to how others feel in the moment" and able to listen and "take other people's perspectives."[23] Self-aware leaders demonstrate a genuine desire to know how others really see them, to admit and learn from mistakes, and to discover and confront their own weaknesses constructively. Leaders lacking emotional intelligence are never more vulnerable than when they fail to see weaknesses that others perceive in their own integrity or character.

Above all, emotionally intelligent leaders display *humility*—a virtue that seems all too rare among powerful leaders in business, government, and other large institutions.[24] Contrast these leaders with the example of Mahatma Gandhi who cultivated humility in his own life and insisted on it in those who would be his followers. The hard truth for today's corporate and political leaders is that humility—which their cultures have tended to devalue while rewarding self-aggrandizement—is a necessary precondition for self-awareness and, thus, for emotional intelligence. As difficult as it is for any of us to live with an attitude of humility, it can be even more so for highly placed leaders surrounded by subordinates who shield them from questions and criticism they may need to hear. Contrary to popular misunderstandings, true humility in successful leaders is seen not as a sign of weakness, but as the confidence to be transparent, able to admit mistakes, and willing to be voluntarily accountable to others.

It is worth noting here that young people have very different expectations of leaders than those of their parents' generation, and it is they who are helping define this new era of accountability. They reject paternalistic, command-and-control methods. They insist on being told not just what, but why. And they demand that leaders listen to them, take their concerns seriously, and respond with candor and substance.

A MOMENT OF OPPORTUNITY

Without question, the 21st century is a time of unprecedented change occurring at blinding speed. Frances Hesselbein, arguably today's wisest and most respected authority on leadership, counsels, "Though time-tested leadership practices remain viable, those practices need to be augmented with new leader competencies" including collaborative learning and problem solving across sectors.[25] The great challenges facing global society today—from the effects of population shifts to the allocation of basic resources—are beyond the ability of any one institution or sector to tackle alone. Leaders in business, government, education, and nongovernmental organizations must learn to work together to map the pathway to a better future.

Such collaboration will require more trust than now exists between many of these institutions. Even so, we are interconnected globally in what Martin Luther King Jr. called an "inescapable network of mutuality," not only because we share a common destiny but also because we have the tools at our fingertips to build understanding and facilitate strategic cooperation. Amidst the fragmentation and instability of our changing world, we are being brought closer together through common technologies, economic interests, and interdependencies.

This moment in time may provide history's greatest opportunity for leaders to engage one another in pursuit of the common good.

CHAPTER 4

Peter Drucker's Light: Illuminating the Path for 21st-Century Leaders

Frances Hesselbein

This is the chapter I hoped never to have to write—the chapter that would mark the moment we said goodbye to Peter Drucker.

We have lost the quiet, powerful intellect, and a warm and generous friend. Peter redefined the social sector, redefined society, redefined leadership and management—and gave mission, innovation, and values powerful new meanings that have changed the lives of leaders in all three sectors.

I have had the privilege of sitting at the feet of Peter Drucker since 1981, participating in the founding of the Peter Drucker Foundation for Nonprofit Management, being one of those fortunate few who, in 1990 and for the next 12 years, could listen and learn from him as he attended Drucker Foundation board meetings and conferences, participated in our video conferences, and advised in the development of our tools and books and videotapes. His philosophy permeated every aspect of our Drucker Foundation/Leader to Leader Institute initiatives, and will continue to do so.

THE IMPORTANCE OF THE SOCIAL SECTOR

Peter Drucker was not a pessimist, but he was very sober about this decade and believed, "It is not business, it is not government, it is the social sector that may yet save the society." This statement challenges leaders in all three sectors.

I study it and try to list all the ways we can work to sustain the democracy, remembering Drucker's "Know thy time," and "the important thing is to identify 'the future that has already happened.'"

Twenty years ago Peter helped leaders understand that mission comes first; if the enterprise is not mission-focused, it will never achieve the results it could have. His messages have equal relevance, today. When Peter said, "Leadership cannot be taught, but it can be learned" or "Leaders of the future ask; leaders of the past tell," some of us have taped "Ask, don't tell" to our calendars.

When, for the first time I delivered my personal definition of leadership, "Leadership is a matter of how to be, not how to do," in a speech at a conference where he, Warren Bennis and I were all speaking on leadership, Peter said that that definition was the most important message in my speech. It has been my leadership definition ever since. That was 1981. Today, in 2006, I believe even more fervently in this concept of leadership. You and I spend most of our lives learning how to do and teaching others how to do, yet in the end it is the quality and character of the leader that determines the performance and the results.

UNDERSTANDING LEADERSHIP

Today, when I share my definition of leadership with college and university students, the emails I receive underscore the relevance of the "how to be" leadership. One M.B.A. student's email message: "I am very good at doing. I do things very well, but I realize that I don't know what it means 'to be.' Could we talk?" As I have prepared this chapter for a book I am honored to be part of, I have just completed a very moving few weeks of presenting two commencement speeches and receiving three awards and it was all about leadership. I gave the commencement speech, "Leaders of the Future — A Call to Action" at St. Mary's University, San Antonio and at the University of St. Thomas, St. Paul on May 20, 2006. It was all about leadership and the students at both universities are the leaders of the future and they know this.

I speak somewhere twice a week and spend one-third of that time on college and university campuses, with these young leaders of the future. When I leave these campuses I am filled with hope. I find this generation far less cynical and with many more young leaders interested in careers in the social sector. They talk about wanting to make a difference, I felt very comfortable in ending my commencement speeches with "to serve is to live."

When I learned of Peter's death, I was speaking at a conference in Tampa, so I returned to New York and flew to California in time to attend the small, private memorial service at St. John's Episcopal Church on Monday afternoon, November 14, in LaVerne. Doris Drucker, their four children and six grandchildren, Bob and Linda Buford, John Bachmann, Claremont Graduate University representatives, old friends, and I were part of the small group of 25 who gathered to celebrate his life. The Druckers' son Vincent, their daughter Cecily, and John Bachmann spoke; there was the liturgy, and the service ended with a quiet, moving singing of "Amazing Grace." On May 12, 2006, there was a great celebration of Peter Drucker's life at the Claremont Graduate University, the Drucker-Ito School and the new Peter F. Drucker Institute.

I remember when I took my first professional position as executive director of Talus Rock Girl Scout Council in Johnstown, Pennsylvania, long ago in 1970. As I walked into the office that first morning I had under my arm a copy of Peter Drucker's *The Effective Executive*[1] for each member of the staff. I had no idea who he was. I just knew his book was exactly right for our work. Six years later when I was called to New York to become the national executive director, CEO of the Girl Scouts of the USA, *The Effective Executive* traveled to New York with me, as did every book Peter had ever published.

Perhaps if I share with you how I met Peter and the influence he has had upon my work, it may be one more story to add to the thousands of how Peter influenced, encouraged, and challenged leaders to be leaders. All of us treasure his wisdom so generously shared.

I met Peter in 1981 when as CEO of the Girl Scouts of the USA I was invited by the Chancellor of New York University to join 50 foundation and other social sector presidents for dinner, to hear the great Peter Drucker speak. I knew that in such a large group I would not have an opportunity to meet him, but I would have the opportunity to hear him live—Peter Drucker, the great thought leader who had influenced the volunteers and staff in the largest organization for girls and women in the world.

The invitation was for a 5:30 p.m. reception at the University Club in New York to be followed by dinner and Professor Drucker's address. Now, if you grow up in the mountains of western Pennsylvania, 5:30 is 5:30, so I arrived promptly at the University Club, only to find myself at the reception alone with two bartenders. I turned, and behind me was a man. Obviously, if one grows up in Vienna, 5:30 is 5:30.

The man said, "I am Peter Drucker." Startled, I responded with, "Do you know how important you are to the Girl Scouts?" He said, "No, tell me."

"If you go to any one of our 335 Girl Scout Councils, you will find a shelf of your books. If you read our corporate planning monograph, and study our management and structure, you will find your philosophy," I replied.

Peter said, "You are very daring. I would be afraid to do that. Tell me, does it work?" "It works superbly well," I said. "And I have been trying to gather up enough courage to call you and ask if I may have an hour of your time, if I may come to Claremont and lay out before you everything you say the effective organization must have in place. We do. And I'd like to talk with you about how we take the lead in this society and blast into the future."

Peter replied, "Why should both of us travel? I'll be in New York in several months and I'll give you a day of my time." And that was the beginning of eight years of the remarkable adventure in learning and exploration the Girl Scouts were privileged to have with the father of modern management.

The great day came in the spring of 1981 when Peter Drucker met with members of the Girl Scout National Board and staff for the first time. Thus began a remarkable journey for us as he helped us answer those Five Drucker Questions:

What is our mission?
Who is our customer?
What does the customer value?
What have been our results?
What is our plan?

I can hear his voice: "If you don't end up with a plan, a good time was had by all, and that is all." The auditorium of the Girl Scout Edith Macy Conference Center at Briarcliff Manor, Westchester County, New York, is named after Peter Drucker.

When I left the Girl Scouts of the USA, January 31, 1990, I bought a home in Easton, Pennsylvania, promised a publisher I would write a book on mission, and was not going to travel so much. However, in mid-March, six weeks later, Bob Buford, Dick Schubert, and I (all of us enormously influenced by Peter in our careers) flew to Claremont to brainstorm a way to permeate the nonprofit sector with Peter's works, his philosophy. The day before Peter was to join us, we brainstormed all afternoon and evening and the result was the Peter Drucker Foundation for Nonprofit Management, a foundation that would deal not in money but in intellectual capital, and that would move the Drucker philosophy across the nonprofit world.

The next morning Peter arrived to meet us not knowing what we were up to. Newsprint covered the walls of our meeting room, and we took turns presenting our wonderful brainchild. Peter listened with no expression; we couldn't tell what he was thinking. Finally, "We will not name it for me. I am not dead yet and I do not intend to be an icon." (He lost that battle.) "We will not focus on me; there are a lot of good people out there and you will bring them in." (Already he had expanded our vision.)

Bob said that he and Dick thought I should be the chairman of the board. After all, I had just left the Girl Scout position and would have time to chair several board meetings a year for the new Drucker Foundation. Peter's response: "You will not be the Chairman, you will be the president and CEO and run it or it won't work." So six weeks after leaving one of the largest voluntary organizations in the world, I found myself the CEO of the smallest foundation in the world, with no staff and no money, just a powerful vision shared with cofounders passionate about bringing Peter to the wider world, transforming a sector that soon Peter Drucker would name "the social sector" because he believed it is in this sector that we find the greatest success in meeting social needs. The rest is history, well documented and alive on our Web site (www.leadertoleader.org), in our 20 books in 28 languages traveling around the world, and in this chapter.

"THINK FIRST. SPEAK LAST"

It is difficult to think about Peter without remembering his gracious manners, the power of civility that was so much a part of who he was and how he did what he did, a "gift of example." He was enormously generous with his time and his counsel. After that first transforming day with the Girl Scouts, he gave us several days of his time for the next eight years, just as he would pour his time, energy, and wisdom into the Drucker Foundation for the following twelve years. We learned from Peter about passion for the vision and mission, and thousands of our members, authors, and participants shared it with a new kind of exuberance as we documented his impact, his influence.

Many of us walk around remembering and trying to live up to his expectations of us: "Think first. Speak last." We remember how at Drucker Foundation Board meetings he would sit quietly, listening to every word, and then at that magic moment respond with the Drucker insight, and in a few powerful sentences clarify the issue, broaden the vision, and move us into the future. Honoring the past but intensely defining the future was one of his great gifts. For example, he wrote that we would see the reunification of Germany when no one else was making that statement. When the day came and the reunification was taking place, he was asked how he could have predicted this. His reply: "I never predict. I simply look out the window and see what is visible but not yet seen." In our tenuous times, when few attempt to "predict" the future, that one statement of Peter's philosophy encourages and inspires those who would be leaders of the future to "look out the window" as Peter did and "see what is visible but not yet seen."

Each of us has a story of our own; all of us are better for having our moments with this quiet, courteous giant who for a while walked among us, with more questions than answers, thinking first, speaking last, as he counseled us to do. From 1990 on, over the next twelve years, as the Drucker Foundation and then as the Leader to Leader Institute, there are hundreds of moments and messages we captured and treasure. Yet for this chapter I should like to focus on his work and his messages about the nonprofit, the social sector, for he did redefine, bring new recognition, new significance to the social sector as the equal partner of business and government. We hear his voice: "It is not business, it is not government, it is the social sector that may yet save the society."

Some of us may remember his seminal article in the July–August 1989 *Harvard Business Review*, "What Business Can Learn from Nonprofits.[2]" (Some were sure it had to be a typo before they read the article, which turned on its head the old view of the nonprofit sector as somehow the junior partner of business and government.) But Peter said, "The best-managed nonprofit is better managed than the best-managed corporation." Peter forced this voluntary sector "to see itself life-size," and he changed the face of the social sector. When Peter came to that first meeting with the Girl Scout National Board and management team, he told us, after thanking us for permitting him to be there, "You do not see yourselves life-size. You do not appreciate the significance of your work, for we live in a society that pretends to care about its children, and it does not." And then he added, "For a little while you give a girl an opportunity to be a girl in a society that forces her to grow up all too soon."

LEADERSHIP FOR THE "COMMUNITY AS A WHOLE"

Three years ago I was writing about children at risk and I called Peter and asked, "In 1981 you said, 'We live in a society that pretends to care about its children and it does not.' Do you still feel the same way?" Silence, then, "Frances, has anything changed?" Always Peter distilled the language until the message connected. Short, powerful, compelling. We never forget his words, and his message about our children grows in intensity. He lived to see the vast proliferation of college and university nonprofit management programs, centers for social enterprise—hundreds across the country and the world. And we can hear his voice, "Management is a liberal art." One last area of massive influence, of the many we could list, is his achievement in bringing business leaders to see the community as the responsibility of the corporation: "Leaders in every single institution and in every single sector . . . have *two responsibilities*. They are responsible and accountable for the performance of their institutions, and that requires them and their institutions to be concentrated, focused, limited. They are responsible also, however, for the community as a whole." One measurable result of how Peter inspired leaders across the sectors to collaborate for the greater good is that collaboration, alliances, and partnerships across the three sectors, building the healthy community that cares about all of its people, became the powerful shared vision of principled corporate leadership and their social sector partners.

On our 15th Anniversary, April 2005, we celebrated Peter Drucker's life and contribution at our "Shine a Light" dinner. "Shine a Light" was appropriate that evening, and is now, for that is what Peter did for 95 years. His light illuminates the darkness, inspiring young people just discovering Peter, our young leaders of the future who are finding relevance and inspiration just as our leaders of the present have found this Drucker philosophy the indispensable companion for their journey. For the Leader to Leader Institute it is not enough to "keep his legacy alive." Instead, we will bring new energy, new resources, and new partnerships to our new challenge. Peter's light shines across the sectors, reaching leaders hungry for Peter's messages that will illuminate, will change their lives, and in the end will move them to define the effective executive, the leader of the future. That will be the living legacy of Peter Drucker: vibrant, alive for a new generation, with new relevance, new challenge, new significance, new celebration of Peter Drucker's life, his influence, and his light that shines anew.

SECTION II
LEADERSHIP CHALLENGES
IN THE GLOBAL CONTEXT

CHAPTER 5

Spilling Sweat, Not Blood: Leadership for a World Without Conflict

John Hume

As we enter the new century and the new millennium, we are living through one of the greatest revolutions in the history of the world. As a result of that major revolution in transport, technology, and telecommunications, we are living in a much smaller world and the peoples of the world are living much closer together and in more direct contact. Thus, we are in a stronger position to shape that world.

One of our major objectives, therefore, should be to take the necessary steps to create a world in which there is no longer any war or any conflict. For that reason we should study major examples of conflict resolution, identify their principles, and create the circumstances to apply those principles to any area of conflict in the world.

The European Union is the best example in the history of the world of conflict resolution, and therefore the means of achieving it should be deeply studied. I very often tell the story of my first visit to Strasbourg when I was elected to the European Parliament in 1979. I went for a walk and I crossed the bridge from Strasbourg in France to Kehl in Germany. I stopped in the middle of the bridge and I meditated. I thought, there is France and there is Germany, and if I had stood on this bridge thirty years ago, just after the end of the second world war, and said, "Don't worry, the historical conflicts of the people of Europe are all ended and in a number of years you will all be united in a European Union," I might have been sent to a psychiatrist. After all, that moment marked the worst half century in the history of the world with the slaughter of millions of human beings in two world wars.

Yet it *has* happened, and as I stood on that bridge I thought that since European Union is the best example in the history of the world of the ending of wars and conflict, its principles should be studied. And when studied it will be found that the three principles at the heart of the European Union can be applied to any area of conflict in order to achieve resolution. That is what I did. So when you study the three principles at the heart of the Good Friday Agreement in Northern Ireland, you will find that they are the three principles at the heart of the European Union. And what are they?

THREE PRINCIPLES

Principle number one is *respect for difference*. When conflict is examined anywhere in the world what is it about? Difference. Difference of race, religion, or nationality is an accident of birth. No person chose to be born into any community. Therefore, why should difference be fought about? It is something that should be respected. There are not two people in any country who are the same. There are not two people in the whole of humanity who are the same. Difference is the essence of humanity and, therefore, it is not something we should ever fight about. It is something we should totally respect. That obviously sounds a very simple statement, but if it were to be accepted in the whole world then it would make a major contribution to the end of conflict. That principle—respect for difference—is the first principle of the European Union.

The second principle is *institutions that respect those differences*. There is a European Council of Ministers and every country has a Minister. There is a European Commission and every country has a Commissioner and staff in the Commission. And there is a European Parliament and every country has representatives in the European Parliament.

The third principle, of course, is the most important one—what I call *the healing process*. The representatives of all of the people of Europe work together in their common interests—social and economic development. In other words as I often say, they spill their sweat together and not their blood. As they have done so, they have broken down the barriers of centuries and the new Europe has evolved and is still evolving.

When the Good Friday Agreement of Northern Ireland is looked at, the same three principles are at the heart of it. Principle number one—respect for difference: The identities of both communities are fully respected in the agreement. Principle number two—institutions that respect both identities: In order to do so an Assembly is elected by a system of proportional voting, not by voting X for single candidates, in order to ensure that all sections of the community are fully represented in the Assembly. The Assembly by proportional voting elects the Government of Northern Ireland as well and ensures that all sections of the people have representatives in the government.

When those institutions are in place, the third principle—the healing process—will go into action and will ensure that the representatives of all sections of our people will be working together in their common interests, social and economic development, rather than waving flags at one another or using guns and bombs against one another. They will be, so I have often said, spilling their sweat and not their blood, breaking down the barriers of centuries as our common humanity transcends our difference. And in a generation or two, once this process gets underway, a new Ireland will evolve based on agreement and respect for difference.

E PLURIBUS UNUM

Those are three very fundamental principles, but very profound and indeed—something that is rarely mentioned—they are the exact same principles as those of the founding fathers of the United States of America.

I first learned them when I went to visit the grave of Abraham Lincoln and saw the summary of that philosophy written there, which, in my opinion, could create peace in the entire world today. That summary, in three words in Latin, also written throughout America is *E Pluribus Unum*. In other words, "from many we are *one*," and the essence of our unity is respect for diversity. When the United States is looked at, the diversity of its people is enormous given the many countries that the founding people of the United States came from. Yet the institutions of the U.S. respect diversity totally. Presidents cannot be presidents for their whole life, only for a fixed period of time. The same principles apply to Governors and Mayors. In other words the leadership of the United States, even though it is an enormous country, work together in their common interest.

That is a philosophy that the whole world needs today. As I have already said, because we are today living in a much smaller world due to technology, telecommunications, and transport, it is a world we are in a stronger position to shape. It is no doubt that the European Union and the United States of America by coming together could give the best and most powerful leadership in shaping the world. The time has come as we enter the new century and the new millennium to create a world in which there is no longer any war or any conflict—no longer a world in which human beings kill one another.

And of course the best way to achieve that is for the largest countries in our smaller world today to work strongly together to promote dialogue in areas of conflict, particularly about the three principles, in order to create a world in which leaders in areas of division will respect their differences, build institutions that do so, and work together in their common interests. I believe that this is the great challenge facing our generation and, naturally, I hope this challenge will be taken up and we will have a world of the future in which there is no longer any war or any conflict. Let us create a world in which *E Pluribus Unum* is a summary of the philosophy of the entire world.

To do so, the leaders of the United States and the European Union should come together to set up a permanent international body whose function is the promotion of dialogue between the different sides in conflict regions, with the goal of getting them to agree to end their conflict, to respect their differences, and to implement the three principles through the creation of permanent institutions that reflect the diversity of the regions. Ultimately these leaders should help all sides agree to circumstances in which they will live and work together.

The time has come.

CHAPTER 6

Lessons from Gandhi's Leadership: Wisdom for the New Millennium

Arun Gandhi

F ew among the 20th-century leaders can measure up to the standards set
by Mohandas Karamchand Gandhi in the practice of ethical leadership. He
not only won independence for India but also ultimately brought down the
British Empire without firing a bullet, which in itself was a remarkable
achievement that could only be done with ethics, morals, and a transparent
sincerity in leadership. Through his example he gave the world an alternative
to violent conflict resolution—a comprehensive philosophy of nonviolence—
the practice of which requires high moral standards.

The answer to the often-asked questions of how and why he succeeded in
his nonviolent campaign lies in understanding his philosophy of nonviolence.
It will be my humble attempt in this chapter to share with you my interpretation of his philosophy and to connect nonviolence (or what Gandhi preferred
to call *Satyagraha*, the Pursuit of Truth) with ethical leadership.

CULTURE OF NONVIOLENCE

Clearly for Gandhi the word nonviolence meant much more than the
absence of war or the absence of violence. He proved that the true practice of
nonviolence is also about people's attitudes, behavior, and relationships not
only with each other but also with nature and the earth as well. A more under-
standable definition of Gandhi's philosophy would be to describe it as the
"culture of violence" that has so obsessively dominated human life for centuries. His life's mission was to help change it to a "culture of nonviolence,"

the only way humanity could be truly civilized. Gandhi preferred the term *Satyagraha* because it gave the philosophy greater breath and depth. He always maintained that only positive thoughts could lead to a positive destiny and he defined positive thoughts as love, respect, understanding, compassion, and other such positive actions and emotions.

He would classify the violence that humankind practices today into "physical violence" and "passive violence", the first being the kind of violence that requires the use of physical force and the latter the kind of violence that we commit consciously and unconsciously when we hurt people through selfishness and insensitivity often without even touching them or seeing them. We are taught from childhood to be successful in life by any means possible and success is always measured in terms of material possessions. We, therefore, succumb to our egos and become extremely selfish. Gandhi set himself very high standards in his practice of ethical leadership, standards that we often find difficult to practice.

His ideal in life was the story from the *Mahabharata*, a Hindu mythology, where Lord Rama is depicted as the epitome of ethical leadership. Even when the action hurt him Lord Rama did not flinch from the Truth. As a crown prince expected to inherit the throne of his father's kingdom Lord Rama was told instead, that in a moment of weakness his father had promised to banish him to the forest for 14 years. Without seeking an explanation or showing any hesitancy or bitterness Lord Rama renounced everything, left the Palace, the kingdom, and his beloved family and spent the next 14 years in absolute wilderness. This sacrifice for truth and for his father's dignity was what impressed Gandhi the most and he tried to model his leadership according to these standards. In fact Gandhi often talked of creating a "Ramrajya" [rule of Rama] in India after independence and people, even some of his close colleagues, misunderstood it to mean he was aspiring to create a Hindu India. Gandhi did not envision Lord Rama as a Hindu deity but as a model human being and when he talked of a "Ramrajya" he meant an administration based on such high ethics and morals.

In the modern world leaders believe otherwise. Ethics and morals are issues to exploit for personal aggrandizement and peace can only be achieved through brute force. Consequently, nations are vying with one another to build enormous stockpiles of weapons of mass destruction. Gandhi believed the peace that is achieved by holding a gun to someone's head is a peace that comes through fear and lasts only as long as one is able to maintain a high level of fear. Similarly impossible is the belief that one can be highly ethical and moral while still being selfish and greedy. The connection between ethics and nonviolence is the same as between a seed and a tree.

CONSEQUENCES OF DISCARDING ETHICS

Let us look at Indian history of a couple of hundred years ago and even something that has happened in the recent past to see the consequences of discarding ethics and morals in our everyday actions and relationships. In 1857, the British Indian Army decided to introduce Ensign Rifles as a weapon of choice. The British were aware that the ammunition for this rifle had to be bitten before it could fire. Displaying total lack of ethics or concern, the British distributed the ammunition that was smeared with beef tallow and pork fat. The former were distributed among the Hindu soldiers and the latter among the Muslim soldiers. It sparked off a violent conflagration that ended in a massacre just as the more recent event where a Belgian Editor decided to publish cartoons depicting Prophet Muhammed as a terrorist. This has nothing to do with the freedom of expression. Gandhi would have considered both incidents highly immoral, insensitive, and totally unnecessary. In the same breath he would have condemned the ensuing violence as being equally unethical, insensitive, and unnecessary.

The bloody revolution of 1857 convinced Indian leadership [prior to Gandhi] that they would not be able to match British power to commit violence. The Indian struggles for independence between 1857 and 1915 were nonviolent but without ethical leadership that abhorred nonphysical violence as much as physical violence. As a result, they met with no success. Gandhi's early experience in South Africa convinced him that violence can only be combated by nonviolence, as hate with love, and anger with compassion. It meant that nonviolent struggle must not only be totally nonviolent but the leadership must also be wedded to a high standard of ethics and morality. Understandably, there was a great deal of anger among the people of India because of British oppression, which reflected in the Indian leadership so that the first casualties were ethics and morals. When Gandhi came to India in 1914 and was entrusted with the leadership of the Indian struggle, he took a leaf from Napoleon's treatise on war—the General who holds the initiative wins the war. Gandhi decided if the British held the initiative of military power he was going to wrest it from them by displaying superior moral power.

At no time in any of his struggles, whether in South Africa or in India, did Gandhi consider his opponents "enemies" nor did he allow others on his side to ever speak of the opponent as an enemy. He always maintained that in the practice of nonviolence there are never any enemies, they are friends who are misguided. General J. C. Smuts, the South African Prime Minister who had to suffer the brunt of Gandhi's nonviolent campaign, confessed to Gandhi in 1914 that he could deal with angry railway employees who struck work because they were angry and hateful and he did not mind using crushing violence against them. However, he said, he had a hard time dealing violently with Gandhi because he was always so loving and considerate.

General Smuts held Gandhi in high esteem because he saw that although Gandhi opposed his policies of discrimination, as a person Gandhi also held Smuts in high esteem. During World War II when the Conservative British Government led by Sir Winston Churchill unleashed a vilification campaign against Gandhi and called him a traitor, General Smuts publicly denounced the British saying he cannot accept any adverse comments about Gandhi. Sir Winston is, perhaps, the only person whom Gandhi failed to impress with his ethical leadership.

Gandhi proved that moral and ethical behavior is inexorably linked to the sincere understanding and practice of the philosophy of nonviolence. Those who claim that nonviolence is a strategy that can be used when convenient and discarded would also believe that ethical and moral behavior too can be used when needed and discarded when not. Gandhi would totally disagree with this point of view. He would say both ethics and nonviolence must become the law of the being so that one becomes imbued with positive thoughts, positive deeds, and positive attitudes culminating in a positive destiny. In other words, to be effective nonviolence must be internalized.

GANDHI'S CHILDHOOD INFLUENCES

Since nonviolence really dawned on Gandhi at the age of 37, does it mean that ethics and morals also came to him at that age? There is no evidence to suggest that ethics and morals have anything to do with genes or the way he was brought up. Early childhood experiences would play a significant role in awakening the good within them and help one to nurture that good. I recall a significant bit of advice that he once gave me saying that childhood experiences and lessons learned in school amount to the acquisition of knowledge. The important thing is how one transforms that knowledge into wisdom. Gandhi looked at life as a staircase to ultimate civilization and salvation, which one had to climb assiduously one step at a time. It must be the commitment of every individual.

To make his point, Gandhi emphasized repeatedly that he came from a very ordinary family. He had the same experiences as anyone else and, also like everyone else, he became a victim of friends who tried to waylay him. From his early childhood Gandhi was interested in ways to free India of British oppression. He was most disgusted to find a Christian missionary standing by the roadside denouncing Hinduism in loud and vulgar terms.

Gandhi writes in his autobiography of how he and his best friend in school often discussed ways to seek independence and the conclusion always was that the British are tall and strong because they eat meat. The conclusion, obviously, was that Indians would have to start eating meat if they valued independence. The proof of this observation was, of course, Gandhi's friend who, being a Muslim, was nonvegetarian. He was, Gandhi concluded, physically bigger and stronger than others and always excelled in physical activities.

All of this convinced Gandhi that he had to start eating meat so that he could successfully fight the British when he grew up. This activity had to be clandestine because his family would be very upset if they found out. To buy nonvegetarian meals he had to steal money from home, had to often eat two dinners, or lie to his mother that he was not hungry. We know how lies have a tendency to multiply. Eating meat led to smoking cigarettes because that, again, was what the British did. More money had to be stolen for cigarettes or, worse still, they picked up stubs from the gutters to salvage whatever tobacco they could and then roll their own cigarettes. This experience went on for about a year and the guilt haunted Gandhi until finally he decided he had to confess. However, he did not have the courage to speak to his parents so he wrote out his confession and one evening, finding his father alone and relaxing Gandhi stole into the room and slipped the letter into his father's hands. Although he wanted desperately to run from the room he found himself rooted as his father read his confession. When he saw tears trickle down his father's cheeks he began to cry too. The father tearfully forgave his son and the confession, the son says, helped cleanse him of the guilt. This experience made him aware that one must be more discerning and not indulge in wrongful activities.

Two women in Gandhi's early life introduced him to spiritualism and, more importantly, the need to be firm in one's convictions. The two women were his mother and his nanny. His mother was a very religious woman wedded to the Hindu tradition but very open-minded and respectful of other Faiths. Like most Hindu women she often took strange dietary vows. The idea is to give something one loves the most and because food plays an important role in one's life the vows she took related to skipping a meal, eating only two items a day, and the one that troubled her son the most was the vow not to eat until she saw the sun. She took this vow during the monsoon season when grey clouds often covered the sun for days. His mother would continue to attend to all her household chores with a smile, cook and feed the family, and never once regret the fact that she could not eat.

As a little boy Gandhi would often sit at the window praying for the clouds to disperse so his mother could see the sun and eat her meal. When on rare occasions this did happen he would scream for his mother to come quickly to the window but often when she could leave what she was working on and come to the window the clouds would have again covered the sun. When this happened she would smile and go back to her chores and tell her son "God does not want me to eat today."

It is important to remember that Gandhi was the youngest of six siblings—two were from a different mother—but he was the only one who was concerned about his mother's vows. This experience taught Gandhi the need to be firm and committed in the practice of anything one undertakes and, importantly, to firmly adhere to whatever one sets out to do. His desire to study all religions grew out of his experience at home. His parents were genuinely interested in learning about other forms of worship and often invited diverse religious leaders to join them for dinner and a friendly discussion of their beliefs. This experience convinced Gandhi that a friendly study of all scriptures is the sacred duty of every individual. Gandhi concluded there is only one God and that different people know God by different names. This, he believed, is the foundation on which the sincere practice of ethics and values is based.

Evidently Gandhi was more sensitive and accepted these little experiences at home, which did not appear to have influenced the other siblings. Gandhi's scholastic record does not indicate exceptional brilliance. He struggled with many subjects yet was more receptive to what his parents did at home. Gandhi, it must be said, made a conscious effort to convert the knowledge that he gained at home into wisdom by his determination and commitment.

When Gandhi claims in his autobiography that there was nothing special about his family or the manner of his upbringing, he was attempting to dispel the notion that the family was extraordinary or that he was exceptionally endowed. He did all he possibly could to convince people that they can become the change they wish to see in themselves. However, he did miss one important point—that the family, especially his parents, was extraordinarily compassionate, loving, respectful, and committed is important to remember. Stories of his father's truthfulness and compassion as the Prime Minister of an important and sizeable Princely State in India are legendary. In spite of wielding absolute authority over all aspects of administration there was not a single instance of nepotism or personal aggrandizement against him. In fact he was the epitome of modesty and compassion; he was known to give freely to anyone who came to him for help. His mother was the same, which is why on the premature death of his father the family was reduced to poverty. They did not save or possess any property that could sustain the family through the difficult times. This might appear to be irresponsible but Karamchand Gandhi believed that someone's immediate need was much more important than his family's long-term need.

It was this positive attitude—love, respect, compassion, understanding, and acceptance—that ultimately became the foundation of Gandhi's philosophy of nonviolence. The world, according to him, is consumed by selfishness and greed, leading to other negative attributes, which, taken as a whole, leads to the "culture of violence." It is this culture that not only leads to conflict, war, and violence but eventually to the deterioration of relationships, exploitation, discrimination, and the hundreds of ways in which we feed the fire of violence in society. Is this attitude inevitable because it is human nature? No, says Gandhi. Instead of putting out the fire of violence we have been feeding it for generations. If humanity makes the attempt, we can change the culture of violence to a culture of nonviolence. Positive thoughts, Gandhi said, lead to positive words, positive words to positive habits, and eventually positive habits to positive destiny.

If anything, Gandhi's life proves that while a compassionate family and early experiences provide one with the means to acquire greatness it is primarily the responsibility of the individual to convert those experiences into something positive. The assumption that someone from a "good" family will necessarily be "good" is wrong. In the modern sense it might be said that a good family would ensure a good education and that would ultimately lead to success. This is true, but only in the material sense. According to Gandhi, material success leads to moral degradation because materialism fosters selfishness and greed.

This leads to the inevitable question: whose morals and ethics are we talking about? There are two parts to this question. The first is the belief that ethics and morals are different in different religions and the second is the belief that what may be good for one is not necessarily good for another. Since ethics and morals, according to Gandhi, have their roots in love, respect, understanding, acceptance, and compassion, they have to be common to all religions. But then, Gandhi would ask who in this world can say that they do not have their own personal code of morals and ethics. Of course those who swear by materialism would be selfish in their interpretation while those who hold morality sacred would look at ethics and morals in the universal sense.

HUMILITY: KEY TO ETHICAL LEADERSHIP

Another important attribute to ethical leadership is humility. Many years ago I met an eminent Indian politician, Dr. Shriman Narayan, who later became the Governor of the State of Gujarat in India. He shared with me a transformative experience that, he said, is important for leaders to remember. He was a scion of a very wealthy Indian family privileged to do his postgraduate studies at the London School of Economics in the early 1930s. When he received his doctorate in economics he was so proud of his achievement that he returned to India full of grandiose schemes to transform India's economy.

"Give me your blessings so I can change India," he told his parents.

An ardent follower of Gandhi his father said: "First seek Gandhi's blessings before ours."

Young Shriman soon headed for Gandhi's ashram in Sevagram, Central India, which was as primitive as a Gandhi ashram could be. There were several hundred families living a simple, nonviolent lifestyle. On arrival, Shriman went straight to Gandhi and enthusiastically narrated his achievements and briefly outlined his grand economic scheme.

"I am here for your blessings," he said expectantly.

After a few minutes of unsettling silence Gandhi said: "Tomorrow morning I want you to join the group that cleans the toilets."

Shriman was shocked. However, he held Gandhi in high esteem and decided not to question him. Instead, he thought as he left Gandhi's room: "I will perform this odious duty and satisfy Gandhi and get his blessings."

Carrying buckets of urine and night-soil to the fields, emptying them, washing the buckets and replacing them for use again is the most humbling duty one can perform. For someone who had not even picked up a glass of water this experience was particularly unpleasant. He just could not understand why a doctor from the London School of Economics had to do such work. Reluctantly, he finished the work, had a bath, changed into fresh, clean clothes, and reappeared at Gandhi's door for his blessings.

Gandhi said: "Not yet, young man. You will have to first convince me that you can do this work with the same zeal and enthusiasm as changing the economy of India. Only then will I give you my blessings."

It took Shriman several weeks to acquire that humility to regard the cleaning of bucket toilets as important as changing the economy.

It seems clear to me that a deep understanding of nonviolence, or satyagraha, is essential to practice true ethical leadership. Without an acceptance of nonviolence, conflict resolution today has become, for the most part, an exercise in futility because the conflict keeps recurring. I fear the same could happen to ethical leadership without grounding it in the philosophy of nonviolence.

CHAPTER 7

A Better Way: Business Leadership for the Greater Good

Ray C. Anderson

If I were asked to introduce myself, I would say simply that I am a husband, the father of two, the grandfather of five, and I am an industrialist. Though some would say a radical industrialist, I can assure the reader that I am as competitive as anyone you know, and as profit-minded. I founded my company, Interface, Inc., from just an idea in 1973 and through the efforts of many fine people it has grown into a billion-dollar global manufacturer, producing carpets, carpet tiles, textiles, and architectural flooring, primarily for commercial and institutional buildings—now, also for the home—with manufacturing on four continents, and sales in 110 countries; successful by any standard definition of successful. I will come back to that word, "successful."

My assignment for this collection of essays is to tell you a story of organizational transformation that produced a new and better business model—and an ethical definition of success.

In 1994, at age 60 and in my company's 22nd year, I read Paul Hawken's book, *The Ecology of Commerce*.[1] It changed my life and my view of the world. It came for me at a propitious moment. Interface's customers, especially interior designers, had begun to ask a question we had not heard before: "What's Interface doing for the environment?" So, I had agreed, reluctantly, to speak to a newly assembled environmental task force of Interface people from around the world, to address this awkward question. Awkward for me, because I could not get beyond, "We obey the law; we comply."

Hawken's book changed that. It landed on my desk at that propitious moment as if by pure serendipity. Without any idea as to what was in it, I started to thumb it. On page 19, I came to an arresting chapter heading, "The Death of Birth." I began to read. On page 25, I found the full meaning of the chapter heading, and encountered four terms I had never before heard mentioned together in one paragraph: carrying capacity, overshoot, collapse, and extinction, i.e., the death of birth. Species disappearing never ever to be born again. I read:

> A haunting and oft-cited case of overshoot took place on St. Matthew Island in the Bering Sea in 1944 when 29 reindeer were imported. Specialists had calculated that the island could support 13 to 18 reindeer per square mile, or a total population of between 1,600 and 2,300 animals. By 1957 [13 years], the population was 1,350; but by 1963 [6 years], with no natural controls or predators, the population had exploded to 6,000. The scientists double-checked. The original calculations had been correct; this number vastly exceeded carrying capacity, and sure enough, the population was soon decimated by disease and starvation. Such a drastic overshoot, however, did not lead to restablization at a lower level, [with just the "extra" reindeer dying off.] Instead, the entire habitat was so damaged by the overshoot that the number of reindeer fell drastically below the original carrying capacity, and by 1966 [just 3 years later] there were only 42 reindeer alive on St. Matthew Island. The difference between ruminants and ourselves is that the resources used by the reindeer were grasses, trees, and shrubs and they eventually return, whereas many of the resources we are exploiting will not.[2]

Reading this for the first time in the summer of 1994, I *knew*—in my heart and in my mind—that this was a metaphor for the earth and humankind. It was an epiphanal moment for me, a spear-in-the-chest experience. I knew, too, that this account was more than a metaphor. It demonstrated a law of nature—as immutable and as sure as the law of gravity: the cause-and-effect relationship between overshoot and collapse. At this moment, humankind is in overshoot, using at least 123 percent of the planet's carrying capacity, probably much more and certainly increasingly, according to Global Footprint Network, sponsored by World Wildlife Fund.

A NEW DEFINITION OF SUCCESS

I read on in Hawken's book and was dumbfounded by how much I did not know about the environment, and the impacts of the industrial system on the environment—the industrial system of which I and my "successful" company were an integral part. A new definition of success flooded my consciousness, and a latent, lurking sense of legacy asserted itself. I got it! I was a plunderer of Earth, stealing my grandchildren's future, and *that* is not the legacy one wants to leave behind. I wept as I read.

Hawken made the central point of his book in three parts: (1) The living systems and the life support systems of Earth are in decline; we are degrading the biosphere; and it is a developing global crisis; (2) The biggest culprit in this decline is the industrial system—the linear, take-make-waste, fossil-fuel driven, abusive system—of which we are each and every one a part; and (3) The only institution on Earth that is large enough, powerful enough, pervasive enough, wealthy enough, and influential enough to lead humankind out of this mess it is making for itself is the same one that is doing the greatest damage, the institution of business and industry—my institution!

I took that message to heart and, using Hawken's material, I made that speech, committing my company to the road to sustainability. Today, I consider this to be its ultimate purpose. I simply said to my people, "If Hawken is right and business and industry must lead, who will lead business and industry? Unless somebody leads, nobody will. Why not us?"

Since then, I have been a recovering plunderer, and an organization of more than 5000 people, daily, is instrumental in that recovery.

I have told that story in much greater detail in my own book, *Mid-Course Correction*.[3] Its title is intended to connote my personal mid-course correction, my company's, and the one I would wish for all humankind.

Now think with me about two very important, extant trends—one bad, one good.

Paul Hawken says we humans are degrading the biosphere that supports all of life on Earth—us, and some 30 million (some think as many as 100 million) species that share the planet. This is a very bad trend. If it goes on and on, unchecked, we will eventually lose the biosphere. But, can that possibly be true? Perhaps, it would be instructive to consider just how a living planet—the rarest and most precious thing in the known universe—could possibly lose its biosphere, its essential livability. We really do not want to believe it could happen or even want to think about it; but you and I, as responsible people, *are required* to think, and if we *do* think about it, we realize that if the day came in the distant future when Earth had lost its livability, it would have happened insidiously, over a long period of time:

One silted or polluted stream at a time;
One polluted river at a time;
One collapsing fish stock, one dying coral reef at a time;

One acidified or eutrophied lake at a time;
One over-fertilized farm at a time, leading to
one algae bloom at a time.

One eroded ton of topsoil, one developed wetland at a time;
One disrupted animal migration corridor at a time;
One corrupt politician at a time;
One new open-pit coal mine in a pristine valley at a time;
One decimated old growth forest, one lost habitat at a time;
One disappearing acre of rain forest, one leaching landfill, one belching
smokestack or exhaust pipe at a time;
One depleted or polluted aquifer at a time;
One desertified farm, one over-grazed field at a time;
One toxic release, one oil spill, one breath of fouled air at a time;
One unremediated brown field at a time;
One political payoff at a time, resulting in one regulatory roll-back at a time;
One-tenth of a degree of global warming, one manipulated river channel at a
time;
One exotic disease vector, one *new* disease, one invasive species at a time;
One perchlorate contaminated head of lettuce at a time. (Perchlorate is rocket
fuel, and it is in the ground water of the San Joaquin Valley of California,
thanks to an industrial "neighbor".)
One chloro-fluorinated or methyl-brominated molecule of ozone at a time,
destroying the ozone ultra-violet radiation shield—something very dear to all
of creation, since every living thing dies without it!

One poorly designed carpet at a time;
One thoughtlessly designed building or building interior at a time;
One misplaced kilogram of plutonium at a time;
One more ton of nuclear fuel waste at a time, looking for a safe and secure
home for 240,000 years (!);
One advance of urban sprawl at a time;
One insensitive or uninformed architect or interior designer or factory man-
ager or manufacturer or developer at a time;
One obsolete college curriculum at a time, teaching the present system of
destruction, and teaching the teachers to perpetuate it for another generation
or two;
One songbird at a time;
One PCB-laced orca, one whale, one dolphin, one trumpeter swan, one
mountain gorilla, one polar bear, one leatherback turtle at a time;
One entire wild species at a time; *and*
One poverty-stricken, starving, diseased, or exploited human being at a time.

That is how it would have happened, and when we make ourselves stop
and think, we know that is how it *is* happening—already, now. The reader

could make a list of what is happening, just as long, and without duplication. This is the first trend, the bad one. It is a long, long slippery slope, and we are on it. We *are* losing the biosphere itself, one strand of the web of life at a time. It is true, it is manifestly wrong, and it will not stop until either we *Homo sapiens* come to our senses, or we, too, are gone and can do no more damage. If we do come to our senses in time, that will happen one changed mind at a time.

A BIT OF HISTORY

Now, let me address the genesis of that mind change, admittedly in a very cursory way, touching on some key milestones.

If we go back not so far in history, we know there was a time when some people, so-called "noblemen," had life and death power over other people. The latter were literally chattel, i.e., property, and the nobleman property owner could do what he pleased with his property, including kill it for expediency's sake, or just for fun, if he was so inclined. Western civilization that eventually changed, as the field of ethics emerged. Ethics is about doing the right thing, and today we know that the power of life and death by one person over another is manifestly wrong.

But what if the "nobleman" of more recent times (the wealthy property owner) owned or coveted a piece of land, the northwestern corner of Wyoming, with the idea of developing those amazing geysers for his own profit, or to keep for his exclusive, personal enjoyment? To head off just such a possibility, the U.S. Congress in 1872, during the presidency of Ulysses Grant, set aside Yellowstone National Park. Later, American President Theodore Roosevelt, under the urging of explorer, mountain climber, and writer John Muir, raised the public profile of Yellowstone and other natural wonders of America. And still later Woodrow Wilson created the National Park Service, to include Grand Canyon National Park, Yosemite, Grand Teton, and many others. (Muir Woods is that stand of redwoods near San Francisco, named for John Muir, who is often credited with being the father of the conservation movement in America.)

Therefore, the notion evolved that ethics should extend to land, especially land of such breathtaking beauty. The ethical thing to do, the right thing to do, was to protect this natural beauty for all people. Today, we know this is manifestly true; it is the right thing to do.

Years later, in 1933, Aldo Leopold,[4] writing about land ethics in a larger sense, observed that what happens to the land in terms of its plant life determines habitat. Habitat, in turn, supports animal life, and the specific habitat determines, even dictates, what species live there; so the field of ecology developed, which is the science of studying the web of relationships among flora, fauna, and even the microbial world that altogether form the web of life.

Then, some really inquiring people began to ask strange new questions, such as, "If the brown bear stopped breeding above 5000 feet elevations, what would that mean for us *Homo sapiens*?"

Out of such inquiry arose bigger questions, such as, "How are humans affecting the web of life, that is, the biosphere"? It is composed of, contains, and nurtures all the living systems and life support systems of Earth—all living things, bound together in a fragile, interdependent web, the intricacies, and complexities of which we have only barely begun to understand. But this we know: we are part of it, not above it, not outside it—a realization that is a hopeful sign of our increasing maturity as a species.

Then, a brilliant and brave woman named Rachel Carson brought such an inquiry (How are humans affecting the biosphere?) to a new level with her exposure of the chemical industry—a human invention and a central part of the modern industrial system—in her landmark book *Silent Spring.*[5] Most people would say that book launched the American environmental movement. Another way to think about it is that Rachel Carson extended the field of ethics beyond people and land to include all the creatures that live on the land, and in the air above the land, and in the waters that cover the land. We know in our hearts she was right to do so. The prospect of a silent spring without the songs of birds brought to life in our minds' eyes and in our hearts the reality of the abuse by the industrial system; and we knew it was manifestly wrong. She gave poignant meaning to the term, "environmental ethics."

She was pilloried by the chemical industry, just as the church had pilloried Copernicus, for saying the earth was not the center of the universe. That giant of history, Copernicus, backed down and withheld publication; she did not. What a woman! She was the quintessential wielder of the Power of One!

As the abuses of the industrial system began to be exposed by this courageous woman, peeling back the onion, the field of ecology was broadened to extend to *industrial ecology*, asking just how bad *is* the abuse caused by this industrial system and what should we do about it? The answer was, pretty bad! And out of Rachel Carson's shockwave came practically all of the American legislation of the 1960s and the 1970s aimed at protecting the environment, including the creation of the Environmental Protection Agency and its regulatory authority.

The regulatory system: has it slowed the rate of abuse? Yes, it has, but has it turned the negative trends positive? My advisors and researchers—and they are among the best in this field—tell me that *not one* peer-reviewed scientific paper published in the last 30 years has said, yes, the global trends are now positive. Though there are exceptions and victories to be celebrated, the overall global trends with the environment are still in the wrong direction. Biodiversity is plummeting. (The death of birth.) The human footprint is growing; and the planet's carrying capacity is not, but, in fact, is declining, being consumed by humankind's unsustainable appetite for stuff.

Nevertheless, the trend in environmental ethics is well established. Today, we see a clear-cut old growth forest and we know, manifestly, that is wrong. We see deformed aquatic life caused by PCBs and we know, manifestly, it is wrong. We read on a label, "This paint contains lead," and we know, manifestly, it is wrong—not to mention, stupid. We see human encroachment on nature more and more, and we know it is manifestly wrong. We see a building that is hogging energy or whose interiors are finished with rain forest mahogany or whose exterior is *two thousand year old* redwood, and we know manifestly that, too, is wrong. And, we see the overwhelming poverty and environmental injustice in New Orleans in the aftermath of hurricane Katrina, in this land of plenty, and we know that that is very, very wrong.

Therefore, this thing called environmentalism is not new and not left-wing whacko. It dates from way back. Though religious conservatives prefer to call it "creation care," or "providential living," it is the same thing. It is an apolitical extension of a very long-term progression in the definition of what is the right thing to do. Progress may occur in fits and starts with occasional setbacks, but the direction in environmental ethics is well established. There is an inevitability that goes hand-in-glove with the maturing of a species—a growing sense of right and wrong, extending to all of creation, including one of humankind's most pervasive inventions: the industrial system. This is the second trend, the good one.

Which trend will prevail: biological decline or rising ethical awareness? I suggest that the fate of *Homo sapiens* will be determined at the intersection of these two trends. I also suggest that what is needed at the fateful intersection of the two determinate trends is a plan that will shift the industrial paradigm.

CLIMBING MOUNT SUSTAINABILITY

So, what about the Interface plan? How are we, one petro-intensive company, approaching the transformation of *our* company? How are we climbing this mountain, called Mount Sustainability? I can tell you the first decision was mine: to determine that we *are* going to climb it, and to articulate this BHAG (this big, hairy, and audacious goal) as a vision for my company; and even when some people thought I had gone 'round the bend, to stay on message, consistently, persistently, year after year, and to put the right people in the roles, and empower them to make it happen. However, the most important decision was made collectively by the people of Interface, one mind at a time, to embrace this challenging vision. As for my own mind, it has spent the years since 1994 in near total immersion in this new way of thinking and the new business model that has emerged.

We began where we were in 1994, with a schematic, showing all of the connections or linkages between Interface and the earth—its lithosphere and biosphere—directly, and through our people, through our suppliers, customers, and communities. We asked ourselves, "What is wrong with this picture?" We asked this when very few, if any, companies anywhere were asking it of themselves.

And, out of that analysis came a plan, in terms of climbing the *seven* faces of Mount Sustainability, to meet at the top—that point at the summit symbolizing zero impact (zero environmental footprint). This plan is the heart of *Mid-Course Correction*. I will quickly sketch it for you, because I believe it offers a template for the entire industrial system.

Face 1

Waste Elimination, Emulating Nature in Industrial Processes

In nature, there is no waste; one organism's waste is another's food. This means revolutionary redesign and reengineering of processes, severing the unwanted linkages to Earth represented by waste streams. We started here, and have made money every step of the way since—for the last 11 years, as of this writing, $299 million.

Face 2

Benign Emissions, To Do No Further Harm to the Biosphere

This means reshaping *inputs* to factories, working upstream. What comes into factories will go out—as product, waste, effluents, or emissions. One objective is to eliminate smokestacks and obviate effluent pipes, and surely to eliminate any net contribution to global warming.

Face 3

Renewable Energy

Renewable energy, focusing on energy efficiency first, then harnessing sunlight, wind, biomass, and (someday) hydrogen—to cut the fossil fuel umbilical cord to Earth—and filling the "carbon gap" with greenhouse gas (GHG) offsets.

Face 4

Closed Loop Material Flows

Closed loop material flows, to cut the *material* umbilical cord to Earth for virgin fossil-derived materials by creating cyclical flows of materials. The technologies did not exist when Interface started this quest. One by one, they fall into place, including beginning the shift to carbohydrate polymers to replace petro-derived hydrocarbon polymers—using corn dextrose as a feedstock to replace fossil fuel feedstocks.

Face 5

Resource-Efficient, Climate Neutral Transportation

Resource-efficient, climate neutral transportation, to achieve carbon neutrality by eliminating or offsetting greenhouse gases generated in moving people and products.

Face 6

Sensitivity Hook-Up

This is the cultural shift, the mind-set shift, to sensitize and educate everyone, *changing minds*—customers, suppliers, employees, and communities, to inspire environmentally responsible actions, (the thousands of little things everyone can do). We want to drive sustainability into the DNA of Interface and to connect in a more meaningful way with all stakeholders, especially with communities on educational initiatives.

Face 7

Commerce Redesign

Commerce redesign depends on getting the other six right. Then it might become possible to redesign commerce and pioneer the true service economy, one that goes beyond *people* selling their service—accountants, lawyers, teachers, waiters—to selling the services that *products* provide, instead of selling the products themselves. In the case of carpets, for example, this means selling the color, texture, design, acoustics, comfort, cleanliness, the ambience, and the functionality—selling service, rather than product, and retaining ownership in the stuff, the means of delivery. This results in giving those products, life after life in closed loop material flows to bring about manifold improvement in resource efficiency by using stuff repeatedly.

Success on all seven fronts (a successful climb on all seven faces) will bring us to the summit, the goal, "The *Prototypical* Company of the 21st-Century"—modeled after nature. What will it look like? If I can put a picture into words, it will be: strongly service oriented by means of products that deliver service, even as nature delivers services; resource efficient, wasting nothing; cyclical (no more linear take-make-waste processes, digging up the earth and turning it to waste); driven by renewable energy (minimized and afforded via efficiency); strongly connected to all constituencies (communities engaged, customers engaged, and suppliers buying into the vision), and to each other within the organization. *An ecosystem, in which cooperation replaces confrontation*, and one that includes Earth in win-win-win relationships.

This prototypical company will be a way ahead of the regulatory process, rendering it irrelevant, taking nothing from Earth's lithosphere that is not rapidly renewable, and doing no harm to her biosphere—emitting nothing harmful. All the undesirable linkages, gone! New, vital linkages, in place. Sustainable and just, an example for all, the new organization is *doing well (very well) by doing good*. It is also winning in the marketplace, but not at Earth's expense, nor at the expense of our descendants, but at the expense of inefficient adapters, competitors who just do not get it. It is growing, too, even in a no-growth world, should we come to that, by increasing value at the expense of the inefficient; with declining throughput of virgin materials, eventually to *zero*. Only zero throughput of extracted natural capital is sustainable over evolutionary time (the true long run). Our goal at Interface is: to achieve zero footprint (impact) by 2020.

Doing well by doing good, doing good by doing well (setting the example): cause and effect, effect and cause, all rolled into one positive feedback loop that is good for Earth. This is how the triple bottom line of Corporate Social Responsibility, done right, will come together in one truly superior and totally legitimate *financial* bottom line, and companies every-where will want to emulate the example. And that is how an entire industrial system will move toward sustainability.

So, how *are* we—a petro-intensive manufacturing company—doing on the environmental front? It is a work in process. Here are a few metrics,[6] comparing where we are today, eleven years into the journey we started in 1994:

1. Net GHG Emissions, down 56 percent in absolute tonnage two-thirds from efficiencies and renewables, one-third from offsets.
2. Nonrenewable, fossil-derived energy used in our worldwide carpet operations, down 43 percent, relative to production; 13 percent of the

current energy usage comes from renewable sources. The goal remains 100 percent renewable by 2020.

3. Water usage, down 66 percent, relative to production.
4. Smokestacks, 40 percent closed, obviated by process changes.
5. Effluent pipes, 53 percent abandoned, obviated. (We want to operate factories that do not need smoke stacks or effluent pipes.)
6. Trees for Travel, more than 62,000 planted, offsetting more than 135 million passenger miles of commercial air travel.
7. Scrap to the landfill, down 80 percent.
8. Eighty-five million pounds of material diverted from landfills and incinerators by ReEntry®, our initiative to reclaim and recycle used products—precious organic molecules, salvaged to be given life after life.
9. Waste elimination, the $299 million of cost avoidance in the first 11 years has more than paid for all the rest of this mountain climb.

Interface customers can now buy climate neutral carpet, meaning no net contribution to global warming throughout the product's life cycle, including its supply chain; and this is third-party certified. We call it "Cool Carpet®."

This reduced environmental footprint is reflected in every product we make anywhere in the world, in some more than others, not just one product here and one there. We are greening an entire company and its supply chain. We simply do not believe anyone can make green products in a "brown" company (Think "brownfield" polluted land). Furthermore, we know we *are* our entire supply chain, as is any other company or organization, no one stands alone.

But, the reader wonders, how are they doing on the economic front? How much is this costing them? It may be surprising, but this entire initiative has been incredibly good for business. It is a better way to bigger profits—a new and better business model.

First, our costs are down, not up, dispelling the myth that sustainability is costly—those waste savings alone!

Second, products are the best they have ever been, since product designers found an unimagined source of inspiration in Janine Benyus' book, *Biomimicry: Innovation Inspired by Nature*.[7] After reading this book, David Oakey, our lead carpet tile designer, sent his design team into the forest to discover nature's design principles: how would nature design a carpet? He said, "Don't come back with leaf designs—come back with Nature's design principles." Therefore, they studied the forest floor and the streambeds, and they came to realize that on the forest "floor," there was total diversity, even chaos. No two things were alike, no two sticks, no two stones, no two leaves.

Yet there was a very pleasant orderliness in this chaos—call it "chaordic." So the designers went back to the design studio and designed a carpet tile such that the face designs of no two tiles were identical. All were similar, yet every one was different, contrary to the prevailing industrial paradigm that every mass produced item must be the "cookie-cutter" same, reflecting society's predilection for perfection.

We introduced this new product with the name "Entropy®" (connoting "disorder"), and in a year and a half it moved to the top of the best-seller list, faster than any other product ever had. The advantages of breaking the old paradigm, insistence on perfection and sameness, were amazing: There was almost no waste and no off-quality in production. Inspectors could not find defects among the deliberate "imperfection" of no-two-alike. The installer could install tiles very quickly, without having to take the traditional care to get the nap running uniformly. The less uniform the installation, the better; so the installer could just take tiles out of the box the way they came and lay them randomly. There was almost no scrap during installation; even piece-tiles could find a place in the installation. Then, the occupant-user could replace an individual, damaged tile without creating the sore thumb effect of a new tile that so typically comes with precision "perfection." Furthermore, there were no longer issues of dye lots; dye lots merged indistinguishably. This obviated the need for shelf stock (extra tiles on the shelf) of the original dye lot. And the user could even rotate the tiles on the floor to equalize wear, the way tires can be rotated on a car, and make selective replacement of damaged areas.

Even with all these unexpected benefits, I wondered if there was not still more to explain the success of "Entropy®." Then I heard of a speaker on the environmental circuit that began every speech by having her audience close their eyes and picture that ideal place of peace, serenity, creativity, comfort, and security—that perfect comfort zone. Then she would ask, "How many were somewhere indoors?" And almost no one would ever raise a hand. We humans seem to gravitate to nature for that ideal comfort zone. I believe Entropy® somehow brings outdoors indoors in a subliminal way, and that is its real appeal. There is enormous power in biomimicry.

In fact, the redesign of our entire company takes its inspiration from biomimicry, emulating as best we can nature's renewable, cyclical, waste-free, sunlight-powered design principles. Surely, this must also be true for the sustainable industrial system.

Third, our people are galvanized around this higher purpose of sustainability, confirming psychologist Abraham Maslow's[8] assertion that at the top of the hierarchy of human needs is self-actualization, which translates into higher purpose. One cannot beat higher purpose for bringing people together, and it happened for Interface one mind at a time.

Finally, the goodwill of the marketplace has been astounding. No conceivable amount of advertising could have generated as much customer predisposition toward Interface as the same people who were asking that troubling question in 1994 have embraced the company for its efforts.

These four advantages—cost, products, people, and goodwill—have enabled Interface to survive the deepest, most protracted recession in our industry's history. With over $400 million of debt and a primary marketplace—the American office market—that declined 36 percent (!) from peak to trough, from 2001 to 2004, Interface might not have survived such a downturn without these sustainability advantages.

A ROLE FOR ALL OF US

As for other companies and industries, I see no other long-term choice for the entire industrial system if it is to survive. Not just our industry, all industries have to make this transition, undergo this transformation, to survive. Those who do not, would not. What we hope to demonstrate at Interface is that it can be done, therefore it must be possible; we hope to be the first, but not the last. We want to facilitate the growing sense of ethical awareness that will move humankind toward survival, not its own "death of birth"; and we hope to encourage the market to demand ethical production of its products.

This is where all of us have a role. We must and we will, *all together*, learn to make peace with Earth, rather than war, for to wage and win *that* war is to lose everything—and we must teach that new type of peace making in our schools, our homes, our churches, and our workplaces.

There is no question in my mind, based on our experience at Interface, that there is a clear, compelling, and irrefutable case—business case and moral case—for sustainability; yet the skeptics remain. So, given the skeptics' reluctance, even disdain, and unwillingness to accept my case, I hereby challenge the skeptics to make their case. . . . More precisely, I would like to hear the business case for:

1. Double glazing the planet with greenhouse gases; and while talking about the cost of preventing global warming, please address the cost of not preventing it;
2. Destroying habitat for countless species, about whose connection to humankind, in many, even most cases, we have not a clue; ecological

ignorance abounds in our culture. Paul Hawken says the average
American can name 1,000 commercial brands and maybe 10 plants;
  3. Poisoning air, water, and land; or disrupting pollination and photosyn-
     thesis (that ought to be a good one!);
  4. Overfishing the oceans to the point of collapse;
  5. Destroying coral reefs, forests, and wetlands (the beginning of the food
     chain that leads to us at the other end!);
  6. Depleting or polluting aquifers on which food production is so dependent;
  7. Destroying the life support systems of Earth.

As Hawken asks, "What is the business case for an economic system that
says it is cheaper to destroy the earth than to take care of it?" How did such
a fantasy system that defies common sense even come to be? How did we—
all of us—get swept up in its siren's song?

What is the business case for destroying the basic infrastructure that under-
girds civilization itself, the natural systems on which everything utterly
depends, including the economy? For what economy can even exist without
air, water, materials, energy, food, *plus* climate regulation, an ultraviolet radiation shield, pollination, seed dispersal, waste processing, nutrient cycling,
water purification and distribution (natural filtration and the hydrologic
cycle), soil creation and maintenance, flood and insect control—all supplied
by nature and her natural systems? The economist would say, all these are
externalities and do not count in the financial system. That is a flawed view
of reality! Without them, there would be no economy in the first place. How
can it be good business to externalize them and assume license to destroy
them by arbitrarily saying they do not count?

I am waiting with bated breath for the answers, so I can correct my errant
ways. Of course, there are no answers, and therein lies the inevitability of
sustainability. It is only a question of how much pain before a growing sense
of ethics gets us off the slippery slope of biological decline, and we opt for
survival.

Who is really at risk here? Not you, not I. Let me introduce you to this
person whom I, myself, met in the early days in this mountain climb. On a
Tuesday morning in March 1996, I was talking to our people, as I did at
every opportunity, trying to bring them along—this time in southern
California—often, not knowing whether I was connecting. But about five
days later, back in Atlanta, I received an e-mail from Glenn Thomas, one of
the Interface people in the California meeting. He was sending me an original poem that he had composed after our Tuesday morning together. When
I read it, it was one of the most uplifting moments of my life, because it told

me at least one person had really "got it". Here is what Glenn wrote, and here is the person I want the reader to know:

Tomorrow's Child
Without a name; an unseen face
and knowing not your time nor place
Tomorrow's Child, though yet unborn,
I met you first last Tuesday morn.

A wise friend introduced us two,
and through his shining point of view
I saw a day that you would see;
A day for you, but not for me.

Knowing you has changed my thinking,
for I never had an inkling
That perhaps the things I do
might someday, somehow, threaten you.

Tomorrow's Child, my daughter-son,
I'm afraid I've just begun
To think of you and of your good,
Though always having known I should.

Begin I will to weigh the cost
of what I squander; what is lost
If ever I forget that you
will someday come to live here too.[9]

Every day of my life since, *Tomorrow's Child* has spoken to me with one simple but profound message, which I, the writer, presume to share with you, the reader: We are each part of the web of life—the continuum of humanity, yes, but in a larger sense the web of life itself—and we have a choice to make during our brief visit to this beautiful, living planet: to hurt it or to help it. For you, it is *your* choice.

CHAPTER 8

Problems of Hunger and the Global Response

E.T. York

The admonition to "feed the hungry" reflects a moral or ethical challenge found in some of the oldest writings, including those of the *Bible*. Before addressing some of these ethical issues, however, let me first examine the overall problems of global hunger and efforts to address these problems.

GLOBAL HUNGER ISSUES

From earliest recorded times, human populations have experienced famine as food supplies have failed to keep pace with need or demand. In fact, as some have put it, there has been a continuing struggle between the "breeders" and "feeders," and all too often the "feeders" have not kept up.

Thomas Malthus, a British philosopher/minister, in 1798, in his essay on the *Principles of Population*,[1] observed that human populations would increase at a more rapid rate than man's ability to feed himself, resulting, ultimately, in global famine, and chaos. Throughout recent history, such a "principle" has appeared to be validated.

Some studies indicate that forty thousand children die of hunger and related illnesses each day—a staggering statistic in a "world of plenty." The World Bank has estimated that over one billion people live in poverty where hunger-related deaths are rampant.

Prior to World War II, food needs were met primarily by expanding cultivated areas. As more food was needed, more land was brought into production. Although there were pockets of hunger in all areas, immediately prior to World War II, every major region of the world was self sufficient in food production except one; and that region, Western Europe, could have produced its food needs had it not placed primary emphasis on the production and export of industrial products while importing much of its food.

Despite the substantial improvement in food production and its availability in recent decades, there continues to be major problems of global hunger and malnutrition. The greatest hunger problems are found in those countries suffering the most from poverty. The two go hand in hand.

UNPRECEDENTED GROWTH IN HUMAN POPULATIONS AND FOOD SUPPLIES

The post–World War II era has seen a major growth in agricultural production as global populations increased at an unprecedented rate. Agricultural output in the last half of the twentieth century grew at the rate of approximately two and a half percent annually. Moreover, during this period, the growth in global food production exceeded the growth in population, resulting in an overall increase in per capita food production of some six-tenths of one percent (0.6 percent) annually.[2]

This growth can be attributed not so much to an expansion of the total area under cultivation, but rather to a greater productivity resulting from the development and application of improved technology. Some have referred to this as "vertical" rather than "horizontal" growth.

This improvement in food output was made possible not only by large production increases in industrial regions, including Western Europe, North America, and Australia, but also in many Third World countries—especially in Asia. Much of this improvement was associated with increases in cereal production, which occurred as a part of the so-called Green Revolution. Yet hunger and malnutrition remain serious problems.

With such growth one might assume that global food supplies would be adequate. However, such statistics are often misleading. Africa, for example, has not shared in this improvement. In the last two decades of the twentieth century, per capita production of food in Africa declined at the rate of approximately one percent annually.[3]

Although average production in the other major regions of the world may reflect significant progress, extensive areas in every region, for various reasons, have not enjoyed the progress necessary to accommodate basic food requirements. Moreover, even in regions that normally have good supplies, temporary shortages and even famine can result from war, floods, droughts, earthquakes, and other disasters that disrupt production.

Today, the Food and Agriculture organization of the United Nations estimates that nine hundred million people are hungry due to a deficiency of calories and protein.[4] Moreover, more than two billion people experience a micronutrient deficiency due to a deficiency of vitamins and minerals.[5] "Vitamin A deficiency, iron deficiency anemia, and zinc deficiency increase the probability of early death for children and women, impair IQ development in children, and lead to a large loss in quality of life, productivity and economic development in developing countries."[6]

A part of this difficulty grows out of the fact that, in many cases, food is not produced where it is needed, and there are not adequate mechanisms or resources to get food to those having the greatest need. A major factor has been the fact that a lack of purchasing power limits the ability of many of the world's hungry and malnourished to buy the food that is available.

FUTURE PROSPECTS FOR AGRICULTURAL PRODUCTION

If the sort of spectacular growth in agricultural production in the last half of the twentieth century has fallen short of meeting global needs, what are the prospects of doing better—of more adequately accommodating these needs?

Current trends in food production do not offer great promise in this regard. Indeed, it is readily apparent that growth in agricultural production in much of the Third World is significantly slowing.[7]

Many believe that the Green Revolution, which saw remarkable progress in cereal production in the last three to four decades, has essentially run its course and that future advances in agricultural output will depend on further significant breakthroughs in the development of production technology through research.

CONCERN OVER FUTURE PROSPECTS

In reflecting on some of these trends, there is obviously good news and bad news. The good news is that since World War II there have been remarkable global gains in agricultural production and food supplies—by all odds the greatest gains in history within a comparable period. The bad news is that these gains have not been enough to address the problem adequately. Moreover, ominous dark clouds on the horizon suggest that the problem could become much worse. Here is some of the evidence to support such a contention.[8]

Population Growth

First, the demand for food is steadily growing as tens of millions of people are added to the global population annually. Significantly, over ninety percent

of this growth is occurring in the developing world where serious problems of
hunger and malnutrition already exist.

Arable Land

A second cause for concern is the growing difficulty in expanding areas
of good, arable land well suited for cultivation. Although such areas are
declining globally, there are still some areas of suitable land that could be
brought into cultivation—especially in Africa and South America. However,
several factors limit its use:

1. Available, arable land is not located where population is concentrated.
2. The lack of infrastructure may limit the distribution of inputs and access
   to markets.
3. Health problems of humans and livestock may limit the development of
   large areas of Africa.
4. In some areas the cost of bringing available land into cultivation,
   including clearing, removing rocks, providing irrigation water, etc., may
   be prohibitive.

These factors are limiting significantly the rate at which new areas are
being brought into cultivation.

Environmental and Natural Resource Degradation Problems

Another and most disconcerting concern relating to agriculture's ability
to achieve continuing improvement in productivity relates to the belief by
many that we are, in fact, compromising the ability of future generations to
meet their food needs by our current misuse of the natural resources on
which agriculture depends.

Nothing in recent years has captured the attention and generated the
concern of the world community more than the evidence of serious global
environmental and natural resources degradation problems. These include
the rapid destruction of tropical forests, the increasing concentration of
atmospheric carbon dioxide and related global warming trends, the destruction of the ozone layer in the atmosphere, as well as ozone pollution problems
near the Earth's surface, major problems of soil erosion, the contamination
of underground aquifers, as well as lakes and streams, acid rain, and myriad
other difficulties.

The World Commission on Environment and Development,[9] chaired by
Prime Minister Brundtland of Norway, issued a comprehensive report on

this subject entitled *Our Common Future*. This report considers how these environmental and natural resources difficulties may impact future development efforts in poor countries.

The Panel on Food, Agriculture, Forestry, and the Environment of the World Commission[10] had this to say about the potential implications to global food systems: "The next few decades present a greater challenge to the world's food systems than they may ever face again. The efforts needed to increase production in pace with an unprecedented increase in demand, while retaining the essential ecological integrity of food systems, are colossal, in both magnitude and complexity. Given the obstacles to be overcome, most of them man-made, it can fail more easily than it can succeed."

Agriculture is viewed as both a contributor to, as well as a victim of, some of these global environmental difficulties. For example, intensification of traditional agricultural systems to meet growing needs can have undesirable environmental or ecological consequences such as greater deforestation, increased soil erosion, and a deterioration of soil structure and fertility. Moreover, the development of more intensive, modern systems may lead to problems of salinity, water logging, and the chemical contamination of aquifers. These environmental difficulties, in turn, may limit the capacity of agriculture to meet growing food needs. These circumstances have led to growing concerns in the global community over the need to consider ways of meeting current requirements for agricultural products without creating environmental or natural resource problems that might jeopardize the ability to meet future needs.

NEED FOR RESEARCH

It is increasingly apparent that if the future food needs of the developing world are to be met, major research attention must be given to the goal of achieving sustainable agricultural systems. Future research must address many factors that constrain or limit the achievement of sustainability objectives. Addressing such constraints will require efforts in such areas as

1. the conservation, evaluation, and use of germ plasm in genetic improvement efforts with crops and livestock;
2. crop management, including fertilizer use, pest control, and various cultural practices;
3. the development of improved and more intensive systems that might evolve from traditional and indigenous systems;

4. soil and water management, including erosion control, effective and efficient use of irrigation water, etc.; and
5. the management of animal systems, including animal health, and nutrition.

OTHER ISSUES WITH RESEARCH IMPLICATIONS

Rapidly expanding global populations have prompted the international donor community to give primary emphasis to research and other efforts aimed at meeting growing needs of developing countries. There is increased recognition that, while it is vital to increase production or food availability, this alone is not enough. People must have the financial means to acquire needed food. Throughout the developing world great numbers of people are too poor to purchase the food they need. Consequently, there is growing recognition of the need to place increased emphasis on efforts aimed at improving incomes of poor people as well as increasing food production.

Food Self-Reliance

Research efforts directed towards increasing food production, per se, might imply that the goal of agriculture in a developing country should be that of achieving self-sufficiency. It is recognized, however, that this might not be the most efficient or effective way of meeting food needs of such countries. Many countries do not enjoy a comparative advantage in the production of some food commodities. It may be advantageous, therefore, for such countries to purchase the commodities from other countries that can produce them more efficiently while concentrating on the production of those commodities for which they do enjoy a comparative advantage.

In recent years, many have suggested that consideration be given to helping developing countries achieve the goal of *self-reliance* rather than self sufficiency. Food self-reliance is defined as "the capacity of the nation to provide a sufficient stable food supply to all of its inhabitants either from domestic production or from production of exportable goods to enable commercial imports to cover the domestic deficit of food."

Nonfood as Well as Food Commodities

With a goal of achieving the capacity for food self reliance, there is logic to support research with nonfood crops, as well as other food crops that have received limited attention. Many of these commodities have the potential for both domestic consumption and export.

Strengthening the export crop sector could not only improve foreign trade balances but also enhance the incomes of poor people so that they can be better able to purchase food they need. Moreover, foodstuffs produced through such operations can make significant contributions to improving the diets of indigenous populations.

More Attention to Less Endowed Regions

There is also need to give greater attention to addressing the problems of less endowed areas that frequently involve fragile ecosystems. It is recognized that progress in such areas will be more difficult and that greater gains will be possible in more favored areas. While efforts should continue in better-endowed regions, the people in the poorer regions must also receive more attention.

It should be recognized that some of the marginal areas have the potential to be converted into better-endowed regions through investments in infrastructure, drainage, and irrigation or other technological innovations. It should also be recognized that increasing the capacities of the more favored areas may help to relieve the pressures on the less favored, more fragile ecosystems.

Certain areas of emphasis should contribute to improvements of less endowed regions, as well as contributing to sustainable objectives, generally. Such research should include, for example, plant breeding to achieve improved genetic resistance to insects and diseases, along with tolerances to stresses such as drought, high, and low temperatures, acid or alkaline soil conditions, low fertility levels, and chemical toxicities in the soil. It also involves research dealing with integrated pest management, including biological control measures and the use of leguminous crops to supply nitrogen to cropping systems.

Biotechnology

The development of new techniques or tools for research in the biological sciences in recent years has given rise to high hopes for the contributions that these tools might make to meeting the growing demands for food in the developing world. The use of such techniques, frequently referred to as biotechnology research, offer exciting potential. However, this needs to be put in appropriate perspective.

Such research approaches are merely new tools or techniques. They may compliment but not replace many existing techniques. They may, in fact, provide the means to accelerate programs in improving developing world food production, but are not, however, expected to represent a panacea that will revolutionize food production and solve the problem of hungry people over night.

A Vital Research Mission

The foregoing material emphasized the vital role that agricultural research must play in meeting the anticipated growth in demand for food. Recent decades have seen remarkable advances in this area. Much of this progress has resulted from improvements in the harvest index—that is, by developing crops which have a higher proportion of the total crop material produced in the part to be harvested (e.g., a higher proportion of grain). The harvest index for improved wheat varieties, for example, has now been increased over fifty percent. What is the potential for further improvements in the harvest index? There are obvious limitations—but how far can we go?

Are there opportunities to improve the efficiencies of the photosynthetic process? Can we significantly improve the rate at which atmospheric nitrogen is fixed and made available to plants? Is it possible to increase the efficiencies with which plant nutrients are used?

What about multiple cropping? Can we make further gains in productivity by shortening the life cycles of crops? Progress in this area has already made it possible to grow three crops of rice in some tropical areas instead of the usual one or two. Can the life cycle be shortened still further to grow even four crops? We normally measure productivity in terms of yields per crop on a given area of land. Would a better measure be yield per day?

What can we do to improve yields and make crops more productive in less-endowed areas or under stressful conditions such as locations with too little or too much moisture, high or low temperatures, low fertility, or conditions of chemical toxicity in soils? Can we develop crops that will be more tolerant of toxic elements in the atmosphere such as ozone? With the prospects of global warming, can we, through research, modify crops so that they might adjust to the effects of such possible changes in climates and mitigate some of the harmful effects that some predict?[11]

An Antiscience Bias

Given the critical role that science must play in meeting future global food needs, it is disturbing to see the emergence in some circles of some of the negative attitudes on the subject. For example, there seems to be a significant "anti-science" bias that characterized much of the "alternative agriculture movement" in the United States in recent years. This is also quite evident in the attitude towards genetic engineering and other biotechnology approaches to improving crop and animal production. Such attitudes are truly unfortunate because the challenge of achieving sustainable agricultural systems that will meet the growing needs of people rests in large measure with research institutions and their development of improved technology.

Science is not the problem. Research must focus increased attention on developing and applying the technology needed to achieve both the economic and ecological dimensions of sustainable food production. Research organizations must continue to explore ways in which agriculture may become more productive, efficient, and economically viable—achieving such objectives in ways that enhance, rather than degrade, the environment. There is no way in which agriculture can meet the ever growing needs of people without the use of modern technology, including the appropriate use of agricultural chemicals which some are suggesting should be banned.

A long-time friend and colleague, the late Orville Freeman, former U.S. Secretary of Agriculture, some time ago sent me a copy of a speech he had given at the World Future Society Conference dealing with the future of the biosphere. The title of this paper was "Humanity versus the Environment." Freeman addressed the basic dilemma of protecting our planet's environment while feeding its rapidly growing hungry population. He referred to those who opposed the use of modern technology to improve food production for fear of contributing to environmental problems and responded to such arguments by emphasizing that humanity's need for food would not be met without the use of modern technology.

I would add that science and technology can and must help us deal with problems that might grow out of the use of such technology.

The issue is not one of "humanity versus the environment." This suggests some irreconcilable conflict, which I do not believe, exists. Perhaps a more appropriate title would be "humanity in harmony with the environment." This is what we must strive to achieve—helping agriculture, and, indeed, all of humanity, to become truly in harmony with the environment.[12]

THE SPECIAL PROBLEMS OF AFRICA

No discussion of world hunger would be complete without addressing the special problems of Africa. Currently, conditions are much worse in Sub-Saharan Africa (SSA) than those found in most of Asia and Latin America. Moreover, the outlook for the immediate future is not optimistic.

What is unique about Africa? Why is this problem more severe there than in other developing regions?

The problems in Africa would appear to include a dearth of vital institutions, basic infrastructure, and perhaps most critical, too few trained personnel to provide leadership in the professions, business, industry, and government.

Another major factor is that most of SSA was under European colonial powers for many years (primarily England, France, Germany, Belgium, and the Netherlands). After World War II, a wave of anticolonialism sentiment, in effect, resulted in the withdrawal of colonial powers long before these under developed countries were ready to become independent. In addition to the dearth of trained personnel and basic institutions, there was virtually no history or experience of governing in these countries. This has often resulted in civil wars, tribal conflicts, unstable governments, despotic leaders, and often a nondemocratic form of government. This has led to chaotic conditions and unstable governments in most the Sub-Saharan countries at one time or another since World War II. Such conditions have had extremely negative impact on development efforts.

In 1997, I was invited by the Carter Center and the U.S. Agency for International Development (USAID) to lead a mission to the troubled continent to explore opportunities to improve food production south of the Sahara.[13]

The Carter Center, under former U.S. President Carter, had been involved in the region for more than ten years with a program to explore ways to significantly improve food production as well as to address major health problems. The program was being supported by the Nippon Peace Foundation of Japan. The agricultural phase of the program was under the leadership of Dr. Norman Borlaug, who received the Nobel Peace Prize in the early 1970s as the "Father of the Green Revolution," which was responsible for enormous improvements in food production in Asia and other parts of the world outside of Africa.

Borlaug and the Carter Center program, through thousands of demonstrations in some fourteen Sub-Saharan African countries, effectively demonstrated that food crop yields could be doubled, tripled, and even quadrupled with the use of a simple and inexpensive package of technology primarily involving improved seed and chemical fertilizers. However, small farmers throughout the region faced many problems that kept them from using and benefiting from this technology.

Our team found a disturbing set of circumstances in the region. Our report set forth a few facts to illustrate the problem:

1. Eighty percent of the world's poorest countries are in Africa. Since 1960 the standard of living of Sub-Saharan Africa (SSA) has stagnated or fallen, unlike in Asia and other continents.

2. The World Bank estimates that half the population of SSA lives below the poverty level and subsists on per capita income levels of less than one dollar per day.

3. Some thirty-million preschool-aged children are significantly malnourished. Unless significant improvements are made there will be a dramatic increase in malnourished children in the region by the year 2020.

4. With a projected average annual growth rate of nearly three percent, the population of SSA will likely triple in the next thirty years, before the rate slows significantly. This is the highest population growth rate of any region of the world.

5. For several decades, rapid population growth has exceeded the growth in food production. Of the major developing regions of the world, only in SSA has per capita food and agricultural production been declining.

6. SSA was a food exporter until the 1970s when it became a net importer. It is estimated that by the year 2020, Africa will need to import about thirty million tons of cereal each year to fill the gap between projected market demands and supply. If all Africans were fed at nutritionally desired levels, SSA would need an additional one hundred eighty-five million tons annually from increased production or other sources.

7. Much of Africa's land is threatened by degradation as rural people put their short-term survival needs ahead of resource sustainability.

8. The agricultural sector dominates the economies of most SSA countries. Despite this, donor assistance declined in the 1980s. This downward trend has accelerated since 1990. Moreover, bilateral assistance to agriculture by major donors also has declined since 1990.

In its report, our team identified the following major problems or constraints that were keeping farmers from using and benefiting from the simple package of technology identified by the Carter Center program:

1. Poor input supply system (fertilizer, seeds, etc.)
2. Limited rural credit available to farmers
3. Inadequate marketing system for agricultural products
4. Weak agricultural extension and research programs
5. Macroeconomic and sector policies that are detrimental to the interests of farmers
6. Poor physical infrastructure including rural roads, railroads, and communication systems, which add to the cost of producing and marketing farm products.

In identifying these problems, our team report called for the international donor community, including USAID, the World Bank, U.N. agencies, and others to provide significant financial support to programs in the region that might effectively address and remove these constraints so that major improvements in food production might be realized.

The G8 Summit held in Gleneagles, Scotland, in 2005 agreed to the following:

> Double aid for Africa by U.S. $25 billion a year by 2010, as well a cancel one hundred percent of the multilateral debts of the highly indebted poor countries and adopt a special package of debt consolidation for Nigeria of approximately U.S. $17 billion.[14]

THE RESPONSE TO GLOBAL HUNGER AND FAMINE

There have been substantial efforts by different groups to address the problems of global hunger. One of the most effective programs has been the Consultative Group on International Agricultural Research (CGIAR), a system of international agricultural research centers dedicated to improving global food production. The CGIAR has enjoyed remarkable success in developing the technology to increase food supplies. In fact, one of the scientists, Norman Borlaug, at the International Center for Wheat and Maize with headquarters in Mexico was awarded the Nobel Peace Prize over three decades ago for his work in substantially increasing wheat production in Asia and elsewhere. The International Rice Research Institute (IRRI) with headquarters in the Philippines, through the development of improved varieties and better cultural practices, has resulted in increased rice production which some estimate may have kept a billion people in Asia from starving. There are some fourteen other centers in the CGIAR system dealing with research to improve food production in the developing world. The system is supported financially by a consortium of donors including the World Bank, U.N. agencies, and many nations, including the U.S.

Programs supported by individual nations have also focused on improving food production. The U.S., through the U.S. Agency for International Development (USAID), has made major contributions to improving Third World food production. I mention only a couple of programs with which I was personally involved.

Shortly after President Sadat of Egypt was assassinated in 1981, Egyptian President Mubarak came to Washington to meet with President Reagan to request assistance in agriculture. Mubarak pointed out that food production in Egypt was failing to keep up with population growth, resulting in his country having to import large quantities of its staple food crop, wheat. This was having a disastrous effect on Egyptian economy.

The Reagan White House responded by appointing a Presidential Commission on Egyptian Agriculture that I was asked to lead. Our group of some twenty agricultural leaders from throughout the U.S. spent two to three months in Egypt, studying the problem and developing a series of recommendations for action.

I presented our report to President Mubarak and his cabinet at a meeting in Alexandria in July 1982.[15] The President gave a copy of our report to his new Minister of Agriculture, Dr. Yussuf Wally. Minister Wally held up the report and said, "This will be our blueprint for action." Fortunately, Wally stayed in his for office over twenty years and successfully implemented most of our recommendations. The results have been dramatic as Egypt has developed one of the most productive agricultures in the world, with world record high yields of a number of food crops such as wheat and rice.[16]

I was also asked by President Carter to lead a Presidential Mission on Agriculture to Central America and the Caribbean in 1980.[17] This mission led to a series of recommendations embodied in the Caribbean Basin Initiative (CBI) introduced by the following Reagan presidency. This initiative has been credited with being responsible for significant improvements in the food production and agricultural economies of Caribbean Basin nations.

Many related initiatives have dealt with efforts to improve the agricultural research and education programs of developing nations. Such efforts had the goal of strengthening the ability of these nations to help themselves rather than to rely on outside assistance.

There have been major programs of direct food aid to address problems of hunger and famine. The World Food Program, with headquarters in Rome, is organized to provide direct food aid to countries suffering from extreme shortages of food. This is a significant, multination humanitarian response to problems of hunger. One of the primary contributors to this program has been the United States.

THE ETHICS OF HELPING THE HUNGRY

There are strongly differing views concerning the moral or ethical responsibility of more affluent societies to help address the problems of poverty stricken, hungry nations. Some of these views have been set forth by Andre and Velasquez[18] in their essay dealing with the moral response to world hunger. Additional thoughts have been advanced by Ford[19] and others. Let me summarize some of these arguments.

Arguments Against Helping the Hungry and Poor

It is estimated that ninety percent of the increase in global population is occurring in developing countries with the highest incidence of poverty and hungry people. Some suggest that helping alleviate hunger and poverty in these countries may actually do more harm than good. It is argued that helping these countries will reduce the death rate resulting in more rapid population growth and increased demand for available food. In the same mode, some suggest that population growth in poor countries will exceed that in the more affluent countries, resulting in even greater hunger problems.

It is also well established that with higher rates of population growth, more people move into marginal areas that are more subject to environmental degradation. This contributes to further deterioration of precious land resources and an ever greater decline in productivity.

It is also suggested that donating food to poor countries may have a negative affect on local food availability by destroying the incentive of domestic producers to increase output because of the competition from donated foods. Such competition has often been found to reduce the prices received by domestic producers for their goods. This has been an all too common situation in many countries.

Some argue that hunger is morally acceptable because survival of the most fit is a law of nature. Others contend that hunger may be acceptable because individuals are not responsible if they are not causing hunger.

Others contend some aid, including food, may at times do little good because it goes to those for which it was not intended. All too often instead of going to those in greatest need, aid is used to benefit the more affluent or the military or it moves into the black market. For example, in Somalia between 1978 and 1984, most of some six hundred million dollars in food aid went to the military and other public institutions. Moreover, eighty percent of U.S. dry milk aid to El Salvador in recent years found its way to the black market with negative effects on domestic production.

Unfortunately, all too often, donor nations' assistance does not go to the most needy countries. In 1988, forty-one percent of all aid went to medium and high income countries rather than to those that needed it most. The World Bank indicated that only eight percent of U.S. aid in 1986 could be considered development assistance. There are many indications that poverty and hunger could be much more effectively addressed by donor nations through more judicious use of development assistance funding.

Many poor countries have not acted responsibly by developing policies and programs to stimulate food production, choosing instead to use precious resources to support their military or for grandiose domestic projects that contribute little to the poor and hungry. Some question why countries that have used their resources more wisely by addressing the needs of the poor and hungry should have to contribute to the support of those nations that have not been so prudent in the use of their resources.

In the same vein, some question the need to aid the hungry because people of means should have the right to use what they have earned.

Andre and Velasquez conclude that "aiding poor nations may be praise-worthy but not obligatory."[20]

Arguments in Favor of Helping the Hungry and Poor

What responsibility do more affluent people and nations have to address these problems? Despite the arguments against helping the hungry, there is overwhelming justification for providing such assistance.

Thomas Aquinas, the Italian philosopher in the thirteenth century, said, in effect, that whatever a man has in super abundance is rightfully owed to the poor for their sustenance.

Children are particularly vulnerable to hunger-related problems. Studies indicate that each week more than a quarter of a million children die from malnutrition and related illnesses. Ironically, many of these deaths could be prevented. It is argued that money spent to advertise cigarettes in the United States would be adequate to prevent the great majority of malnutrition related child illnesses and deaths.

There are many compelling arguments for helping the hungry and poor. In fact, all the major religions of the world have this as a primary tenant. Much of our culture's ethical values about hunger are influenced by the Christian doctrine of love, forgiveness, and compassion. The Lord's Prayer implores God to "gives us this day our daily bread," and many other references throughout the *Bible* deal with helping the poor and feeding the hungry. Charity to the poor is also one of the pillars of the Islam religion.

Mother Teresa of India said, "If you can't feed a hundred people, then feed just one." Some contend that hunger is morally unacceptable because the pains suffered by the hungry out weigh the pleasure enjoyed by the well off.

Helping poor nations address their food needs may involve some sacrifice by the more affluent. However, some contend that to ignore the problem of starving people is as morally wrong as failing to save a drowning child because of the inconvenience of getting one's clothes wet.

Others contend that more affluent, Western nations have an obligation to address hunger problems because our culture has contributed to, and benefited from, conditions that helped to produce hunger through such things as colonization, aid to corrupt allies, and global economic dominance.

The philosopher, Peter Singer,[21] contends that allowing a person to die of hunger has the same moral implications as killing another human being. He also argues that if an individual chooses to spend money on luxury items rather than giving it to a relief agency, which could have used it to prevent deaths from starvation, that person is morally responsible for those deaths.

There are many other reasons for helping poor nations overcome poverty and hunger. There is much evidence to indicate that population growth rates decline as poverty and hunger are reduced. As people become more affluent there is less need for large numbers of children to provide support for their parents as they grow old. Moreover, a decline in infant mortality is associated with a decline in birth rates and reduced population growth rates.

There is abundant evidence that appropriately targeted aid can be very beneficial. For example, U.S. aid to Taiwan resulted in a remarkable revitalization of that country's economy following World War II. This was associated with a marked reduction in hunger and poverty. Moreover, aid to Indonesia contributed to a reduction of that country's poverty rate from fifty-eight percent to seventeen percent in less than a generation.

There are no indications that the problems of poor and hungry people are becoming less serious. Indeed, all indications suggest they will continue.

The moral obligations to respond to these needs are set forth by Peter Singer who said, "I began with the assumption that suffering from lack of food, shelter, and medical care are bad ... my next point is this: If it is within our power to prevent something bad from happening, without thereby sacrificing anything of comparable moral importance, we ought, morally, to do it."[22]

Joachim von Braun, Director General of the International Food Policy Research Institute, very effectively addressed the issue of ethics in a global food system.[23] In summary he said, "Without a focus on ethics, we lose an important means of applying pressure for change and narrow our understanding of why we struggle to end hunger. In the context of an emerging consensus on global issues focused on human dignity, rights, and equity the specific issue of ending hunger needs to be emphasized."

Norman Wirzba summarizes the situation well when he said when it comes to conquering hunger, "we have what we need to make our way—a world blessed with abundance. What we still await is a culture directed to the just production and sharing of this blessing."[24]

Technological advances have contributed to major improvements in food production, especially in the last half of the 20th century. In fact, there are many indications that we have the ability to remove the scourge of hunger and famine from the face of the Earth. However, modern society has yet to meet the ethical challenge of using this knowledge and ability. This is the great moral challenge of our generation.

SECTION III
THE PROMISE OF HIGHER EDUCATION

CHAPTER 9

Ethical Leadership in a Global Society: (*How*) Can Universities Lead?

Beheruz N. Sethna

According to the American Council on Education data for the Fall of 2001, there were approximately 16 million students in institutions of higher education across the United States.[1] Today, almost five years later, that figure may well be in the range of 18 million students. This estimate presents an awesome opportunity and an awesome responsibility. We have the opportunity to influence 18 million young (and not so young) minds and help them obtain the tools for ethical leadership in America—and, because America still is in a leadership position in world higher education—in the world. The phenomenal growth in population, in technology, in knowledge, and unfortunately, in conflict and terrorism, and the ramifications of changes in economics, governance, and resource management have made the task more challenging but more necessary. The messages we send through our daily, tactical, and strategic operations will have an impact—for better or worse—on future generations.

Some might say that, by the time students get to college, they are already ethically fully formed. Although there is some truth to that, it would be absurd to deny that there is some influence on students of the college experience. It is likely that we will not change those at the extremes. Those who grew up believing, or were taught at a tender age, that greed is good and that the end entirely justifies the means, are probably not likely to be positively influenced to a great extent through their college experience. And, fortunately, the saintly people who walk among us, the potential Mother Teresas, are unlikely to morph into executives who raid corporate funds for their own private benefit. However, the vast majority of students—those who have neither horns nor halos on their heads at the age of 18—*are* likely to be influenced by what they hear and see and experience and are taught in colleges and universities in the four, six, or eight years that follow.

So, I do believe that we—the faculty, staff, students, supporters, alumni, administrators, funding partners, contributors, legislators, and publics who influence higher education—have an awesome responsibility to the students who will soon be in positions of leadership in our communities, our states, our country, and our world. The "business" or objective of higher education has traditionally been referred to as "teaching, research, and service." I would rather think of the "business" or objective of higher education as *Changing Lives*. Indeed, my talks to my colleagues at the University of West Georgia consistently stress this message. Those of us who teach the Arts, the Sciences, Business, or Education, or do exciting research in our fields, or do service to our communities and our professions, or award financial aid, or help facilitate student life or residence halls on campus, or operate and maintain our physical plant, or manage fiscal affairs, or create programs to engage alumni and have advancement initiatives, and many, many other activities, change lives. We change the lives of our students, of their children (many yet unborn), of their extended families, of their communities, their states, their country, and their world.

That is what we do—and so, we must do it well.

As one who has combined an academic career with forays into the corporate world with multinational companies, I am at the same time proud of our successes and embarrassed at our shortcomings, delighted with steps forward, disheartened with some negative trends, optimistic about our considerable potential, and concerned about the factors that may hinder our tapping it.

This essay is about our own fortitude, our own courage to do the right thing. The courage to stand tall and true when we need to do so and—equally important—the courage to ask the tough questions of ourselves, and the courage to change when change is best. Former Chancellor of the University System of Georgia, Steven Portch, used to say, "It's easier to change the course of history than a history course!" If we want the corporate, legislative, and public world to respect our courage to stand up to undue pressures for change that is not best for the greater good, we must have the courage to embrace change that is.

Later in this essay, then, I will touch upon some of the ethical dilemmas higher education and its constituencies face, because, unless we can face up to these demons, we cannot be the beacon of ethical leadership for the rest of the country and the world.

Let me start with the question asked at the Fourth Annual Summit Conference (April 6, 2006) hosted by the RTM Institute for Leadership, Ethics, and Character, on Ethical Challenges in a Global Society: *How* (emphasis added) Can Universities Lead? The first part of this essay is devoted to that question—the challenges confronting us in providing such leadership.

However, be forewarned: I will then ask more interesting questions about whether we (universities) have the moral right and the capacity to lead this initiative to address ethical challenges in a global society. If we in the Academy do not ask these questions, someone else will.

ETHICAL LEADERSHIP IN A GLOBAL SOCIETY: HOW CAN UNIVERSITIES LEAD?

In this section, I draw heavily on the work of Peterson[2] and Friedman.[3]

The "Seven Revolutions" proposed by Peterson are described in Chapter 1 of this book; they include population, resource management, technology, knowledge and information, economic integration, conflict, and governance. A few significant conclusions are summarized below because they are relevant for further discussion.

Peterson makes several excellent points in his essay about the changing nature of the world's population. The population of the world is increasing, it is increasing at a decreasing rate, and it is increasing *differentially*—in many ways. The population of many developed countries is decreasing, while the population of the developing world is *increasing* significantly. This has serious implications for resource management and governance. Further, there is an *age* differential—the population of the developed countries is getting older—some like Japan and Germany, much older—while many developing countries will have an increasing proportion of young people. If these youth do not have jobs and education, this has profound implications for conflict. In addition, the populations of developing countries will increasingly be in *urban* centers, which are already unable to support these increasing populations. This in turn has implications for governance and conflict, as Peterson shows.

To amplify these differences, let us consider an economic integration finding of Peterson's: "The accumulated wealth of the 225 richest individuals in the world is equivalent to the combined annual revenue of 2.7 billion people at the bottom of the global income ladder."[4] Again, this differential has enormous consequences for conflict and resource management.

Further complicating the population trends are technology developments that lead to his conclusion that, for children "under the age of ten, the introduction of genetic medicines and therapies could help many of them live to be 120 years old, maybe older." So, not only will key populations increase, but people will live longer, placing even more strains on the resources of the future.

Peterson states, "Eight countries—Bangladesh, China, India, Nigeria, Pakistan, the United States, Ethiopia, and the Democratic Republic of Congo—will account for one-half of all world population growth through 2050."[5] An interesting followup question: How many of these countries are vibrant functioning democracies, and what are the implications of that political reality for them and for the rest of the world?

Knowledge, information, and technology have the potential to level the playing field somewhat. Like Friedman, Peterson postulates that "advances in technology have not only increased the scope, speed, and efficiency of business operations worldwide, but they have also brought down the costs of distance by gradually eliminating the burdens of communication, geography, transportation, language, and even time. The result has been a staggering increase in the cross-border flow of goods and services." He points out "advances in technology have expanded information flows, spanned geographies, reduced time lags in communication, and opened new opportunities faster than ever before." The United Nations Development Program maintains that "developing countries have achieved in 30 years what the industrialized nations took 100 years to accomplish." These benefits are particularly felt in more outward-looking countries. "A recent World Bank report documents how those countries that opened their economies—the 'new globalizers'—experienced a five percent increase per year in per capita GDP relative to non-globalizers . . . "[6]

Before I segue into Friedman's work, let me suggest an eighth revolution that will—particularly if we do not help manage it—drive much of the world of the future, and that is *Religion*. Or, rather, the use or abuse of religion by politicians and "leaders"—and even the masses—for their own ends. (See, for example, my piece reproduced in Appendix A.)

Friedman describes ten "flatteners"—from the fall of the Berlin Wall and the creation of Windows to the ubiquitous iPods of today. These ten flatteners occurred during a 12–14 year period—a veritable blink of an eye. Further, Friedman says, "the convergence of the ten flatteners begat the convergence of a set of business practices and skills that would get the most out of the flat world"—and similarly of professions with different skill sets. And finally, with the advent of China, India, and other countries into this new world, almost 3 billion people who had been left out of the business climate were now in.[7]

These global changes are essentially unstoppable. So, how do Americans fit best into this new world? How do we prepare our children and young adults to survive and succeed in the new flat world?

Education is the key—if we do it right. Friedman describes three "Dirty Little Secrets"[8] of which we need to be cognizant:

1. *The Numbers Gap*: Since the time we won the race to the moon, the number of scientists and engineers has steadily declined in America. Most of our scientists and engineers are 40 years old or older, and the inflow is not keeping pace with retirement. Friedman refers to a study at Boston College that showed that 44 percent of eighth graders in Singapore and 38 percent in Taiwan scored at the most advanced level in math tests, but only seven percent in America did so. He estimates that it takes about 15 years to create an engineer (from interest to graduation)—so we had best get started now.

2. *The Ambition Gap*: Friedman says, "Here is the dirty little secret that no C.E.O. wants to tell you: they are not just outsourcing to save on salary. They are doing it because they can often get better-skilled and more productive people than their American workers." He adds, "When they send jobs abroad, they not only save 75 percent on wages, they get a 100 percent increase in productivity." People in China and India are hungry for American jobs and business opportunities.

3. *The Education Gap*: It should not be the call centers going abroad that worry us. Today, many of the high-end research jobs are going abroad, and of those high-tech jobs that remain in America, many are going to people from other countries. As Friedman says, other countries are not racing us to the bottom; they are racing us to the top. In 2003, Leslie Stahl of *60 Minutes* spoke "about a university that may be the hardest school in the world to get into. It's called IIT- Indian Institute of Technology. A stunning percentage of CEOs and innovators in the American high tech industry were graduated from IIT." As Friedman claims, "Remember, in China when you are one in a million, there are 1,300 other people just like you. The brainpower that rises to the Microsoft research center in Beijing is already one in a million."

In an increasingly "flat" world, many future career paths will be impacted. Higher Education has a special responsibility to increase the probability that our students are provided those abilities such that their futures are secure—called "untouchable" in Friedman's lexicon. Friedman defines four categories of those with untouchable jobs:[9]

1. *Special* people such as Barbra Streisand and Michael Jordan—if you are one of those, you are okay;

2. *Specialized*: "specialized lawyers, accountants, and brain surgeons, to cutting-edge computer architects and software engineers, to advanced machine tool and robot operators." Here, I respectfully but strongly disagree with Friedman. These jobs are by no means untouchable. They are already going overseas and will continue to do so. A recent *60 Minutes* episode spoke of people going to India and other Asian countries for heart and other complex surgeries. Firms in India and other countries do your tax returns, legal work, and software work already. These jobs are not untouchable;

3. *Anchored*: such as barbers, waitresses, plumbers, etc. These jobs cannot be outsourced, this is true. So, if such is the career path chosen, it is reasonably secure. But this is not the main business of universities;

4. *Really adaptable*: This is the one that I personally really believe in. As the world changes, Friedman says, "adaptable people will always learn how to make some other part of the sundae. Being adaptable in a flat world, knowing how to 'learn how to learn,' will be one of the most important assets any worker can have, because job churn will come faster, because innovation will happen faster." This is what the University of West Georgia and other similar institutions are all about. The objective of higher education goes far beyond technical knowledge—it teaches students to learn how to learn, so that, if or when their jobs become obsolete, they can shift gears and adapt to the new environment.

The implications of the changing world for America are many and varied. First, we need to have adequate preparation—in curriculum, attitudes, work habits, etc.—at the middle school, high school, and college levels, to prepare America for the intense competition that results from a flatter world. Correspondingly, legislators, and business leaders would be well served to recognize what an invaluable asset higher education is and how critical it is to our future, and be supportive.

In an increasingly "flat" world, higher education is critical to America's future—Friedman lists several "secrets of American sauce"—things that have made America great and still give us a strategic advantage over other countries. First among these "secrets of American sauce" is American higher education. We need to step up our advocacy for higher education. India and China have realized that education and higher education are the keys to success. They are rapidly increasing their emphasis and budgets as a percentage of public expenditures, as we, as a nation, may be decreasing ours.

Let us also briefly examine some implications of a flatter world for industry and society. A significant result of a flatter world is with regard to the awareness of what is going around in the world outside us. Partly tongue-in-cheek, it almost seems that Americans never got over the European "flat world" theory of the 15th century. Before Columbus, the prevailing opinion was that the world was flat and that he would fall off the surface of the earth. Well, he proved the flat world theory wrong. For most of the 20th century, many Americans seemed to believe that *they* would fall off the surface of the earth if they ventured (mentally or physically) beyond our shores. Children in China, India, and the rest of the world know a great deal about America. When I was a kid in India, I studied American history and government, and learned about American culture from movies and comic books. How much do American kids know about other countries? How much do American adults know about other countries? Aside from war time information, that is. Ambrose Bierce once said, "God uses war to teach geography to Americans!"

We cannot ignore other countries and cultures any more—we are already way behind the game. Not just for reasons of military intelligence, but for business intelligence as well. We need to embrace the flattening of the world. As Friedman says, "Either you get flat or you'll be flattened by China." We cannot maintain global leadership without a global-looking culture. How global is our culture? Even more importantly, what are we doing about it?

As an exercise, if we were to examine the legislative agendas of the 50 states and the federal government, would we find a high percentage of legislatures debating actions and policies to help us be more globally aware and competitive? Or, is more legislation being proposed that is making us more insular and less welcoming to others? Are more legislatures increasing education budgets as a percentage of their expenditures? Or, is higher education accounting for a declining share of expenditures? Are more legislatures looking forward and planning for the complex and diverse world of 20 years from now? Or, are more of them looking backward and doing their best to preserve old ways and old habits—because they are afraid of the impact of more diversity, or perhaps because they blame diversity for all the ills of modern America?

Friedman tells the story of the last national election in India[10] when the ruling party that had presided over good economic growth was swept from power, largely because of the discontent of rural voters. Here's the point: Rural India was not saying, "Stop the globalization train, we want to get off." They were saying, "Stop the globalization train, we want to get on, but someone needs to help us by building a better stepstool." Rural India, living in poverty and with low levels of education, "gets it"—they *want* to embrace the rapid changes going on the world. Does rural America get it? Does rural

America want to embrace the rapid changes going on the world? Do our leaders—at all levels and of all types—get it?

Are we willing to change? Or, are we too afraid of the new world that comes from change?

To be fair, not everyone agrees with Friedman's approach. John Gray has written a counterpoint in *The World Is Round*. He claims that Marx and Engels, in *The Communist Manifesto*, prophesied the end of Capitalism—and look what happened. My response is that there is a huge difference here. They were postulating a different system. India and China are not saying they have a better system. They are saying that we do. They are saying: America, you have the right formula—you did it so well, but you have forgotten your own philosophies of support for higher education, of hard work, of science, math, and engineering. We will use *your* winning formulae of the 1950s and 1960s to do well.

Another criticism of Friedman's work is to refer to the example of the 1970s and Japan. Japan was predicted to take over the automobile world—and "nothing happened." Well, just ask the automobile manufacturers. Japan did not win world domination, but those developments changed the lives and lot of American car companies. So, it is not world domination that is troubling me, it is losing significant ground, and making America less competitive and our business and educational climates much more difficult.

I do not believe that this is a matter of world domination. I do not believe that the world is really flat, nor does Friedman. I do believe that China and India have many, many problems of their own and have a long way to go. I do believe that American scientific research papers still far outstrip those in China (we do not know how many American scientific research papers are being written in America by those of Chinese origin, but that is a question for another day). Having said all that, however, I do believe that we should be very concerned.

Here's the bottom line: Friedman asks: "Are we preparing our children for the race ahead?" And he answers: "No."

It is a flatter world out there. Are we going to get serious about it?

So, how can Universities lead us to a better future—whether "us" is defined as Americans in a global world, or the people of the world? From the preceding discussion, the answer is reasonably clear, though it may not be the entire answer:

1. Education to help our children become increasingly prepared for the future, and to help the people of the world open their eyes to developmental opportunities rather than conflict;

2. Research and development to help with the problem of resource management and economic integration;
3. Helping people, communities, societies, states, and nations be in a position to receive some of the benefits of the 21st century.

In these bullets, I clearly see the traditional missions of Teaching, Scholarship and Research, and Service. So, it certainly appears that universities are qualified, through their traditional missions—augmented by new and fresh thinking—to be a major part of building a better and more ethical future.

And now to the more provocative questions:

Can Universities Lead? Do universities have the human and fiscal resources, the knowledge and the competencies necessary to play the ethical leadership role in a global society?

Can *Universities* Lead? What is it about universities that make them uniquely qualified to lead this effort? Are there challenges—in fact or in perception—to universities playing such a role? Do universities have the necessary authority, standing, and relationships?

Can Universities *Lead*? Even if we assume that universities will play a part in this process, how are they qualified to lead the effort? Do universities see themselves as leaders? Do others see them as such? Do they currently act as leaders among institutions in society? Can they exercise leadership in society if they choose to do so?

Why do I raise these questions? Because, before we assume a leadership role in dealing with *ethical* challenges, we need to get our own house in order. Otherwise, others will ask, "How dare you talk to us about ethics and ethical leadership?" Some soft spots in our underbelly are described below—there are others, but I have selected three to discuss in some detail. Not all of them are the "fault" of higher education, but we are at least complicit in many of them.

THE MESSAGES WE SEND: WHAT'S COOL AND WHAT'S NOT

If we in higher education believe that education is a critical need for the future, I would venture to say that the ethical thing to do is to send this message. Conversely (assuming that we do believe in the value of higher education), *not* to send such a message for reasons of "going with the flow" with our children, our students, our neighbors, our communities, and our funding partners, is not indicative of true ethical leadership in our society.

I would respectfully suggest that "we" (used in the broadest sense) do not consistently send the right messages to our constituencies. If this is so, it is doubly problematic. For an entity to have the ability to send the right messages and yet not do so represents a failure of ethical leadership. If we have access to 16–18 million students at the college level and, through our K-12 partners, far more at the pre-college level, and yet miss the opportunity to convey the important messages to them, is this true leadership?

We are sending the wrong messages to our kids. How many messages each week from all personal and mass communication sources do they hear saying "Life is real, life is earnest, and you better work hard—really hard—to succeed. Go to College; Graduate from College"? Contrast this with the number of messages they hear saying, "Life is a ball. How can we make it more enjoyable for you, with more alcohol, faster cars, more expensive stuff (implying more odd jobs to pay for these, and therefore fewer hours in academic pursuits)?"

Why do I place such emphasis on graduation from college? There is a very significant body of national data published by the Atlanta Regional Council for Higher Education (with a grant from the Woodruff Foundation) that shows that the following variables and more show strong correlations with graduation: Income, Employment Opportunities, Net Worth, Business Ownership, Investment Accounts, Senior Citizens with Health Insurance, Public Assistance (negative), and Incarceration Rates (negative). Let me up the stakes: the following variables for students show strong correlations with College Education of *Parents*: Enrollment in College, SAT Scores, Computer Ownership, Dropout Rates from High School (negative), and Expulsion/Suspension from School (negative). The biggest jumps (benefits) come when one or both *parents* hold a Bachelor's degree. There is a generational effect!

These are incredibly compelling and important facts. Are these the messages we are sending to our children? No.

Perhaps a few times a year, U.S. print and television media report how poorly American children fare on standardized or comparative tests relative to children from other developed countries. About as often, stories appear about poor SAT scores in one state or another. And on a few other occasions, the news media publicize survey results demonstrating that many Americans, usually adults, cannot identify their home states or answer the most rudimentary questions about national or world affairs.

For the better part of the year, however, news stories about students—whether in high school or college—are not about academic activities at all. They are about what "really counts"—athletics. Check out several issues of your favorite newspaper or a few TV news programs, and count the number and length of sports stories. Compare those with the stories about one school beating another in an academic competition or debate, or students excelling in their studies.

I am a marketing professional; I understand about advertising dollars being spent to sell products. But that means we have to work even harder to send messages of long-term relevance, rather than instant gratification. Why are we surprised that Americans do not pay more attention to academics and intellectual activities?

Almost every newspaper has a sports section and most television news programs have a sports segment. How many have an equally regular academic section or segment? Let us not compare apples and oranges here. True, there sometimes are education editors who discuss education issues. But, there are at least two major differences between sports sections and the few academic sections that can be found. The first is that the number and length of athletics stories are an order of magnitude higher than those of academic ones. The second difference is that the athletics stories are generally brag stories, while those academic stories that do appear typically are about how bad things are.

Let us compare apples and apples. Most stories in sports sections or segments are not about scandals—in fact, scandals in sports, as in academics, frequently graduate to the front page. Neither do most sports section stories focus on serious issues confronting the future of athletics—many of those might rate a small subcolumn on the back page. Instead, most stories in sports sections or on local and regional TV channels are about college or high school sports—they are about wins and losses, and one school doing better than another and winning competitions. And, if there is no national or state record broken that week or that day, there are still stories about athletic accomplishments—if those are local or modest, so be it.

For the record, I think that is great—I would not change that; athletics are wonderful and athletic achievements should be encouraged and applauded at all levels. In addition, I want to be very clear that there is nothing inappropriate about news coverage of academic deficiencies. There is no question that education needs to be held accountable and that shortcomings need to be discussed. I am not at all critical of such scrutiny. I am critical of the omission of what else should be reported.

The Times of India (by some accounts, the largest English language newspaper in the world), has a *weekly* supplement or insert of four to eight full-size pages, called *The Education Times*, devoted to stories about education, higher education, math problems, hints on college application and readiness, and so on. How many American newspapers do the same?

I am talking about routine coverage of academic accomplishments, reported with equal fervor as sports stories, if not exactly equal space and time. It would not be difficult to find such stories. Remember that most athletics stories are not about national champions. Week after week, the news media publish stories on local and regional athletics competitions. Is the coverage of the local debate competition or the science bowl the same as that of the local football game and the detailed description of the touchdowns? Let us use the same standard for stories on academics. Let the kids, their parents, and the adults who influence them, read about local academic successes with the same frequency they read about those in athletics.

I am not claiming that the *entertainment* value of a science competition or debate is the same as that of a football game, or that equal time be given to broadcasting an entire debate tournament as is given to a football game. I merely make the claim that *the news* should go a little beyond pure entertainment value—and give approximately equal time (or some reasonable fraction thereof) to coverage of positive occurrences in academics.

Neither am I implying that stories about academic successes will, by themselves, improve classroom teachers, and test performance. Those of us in education must continuously work harder and smarter to improve what we do. But just as it would be naïve to imply that a significant increase in media reporting will make up for shortcomings in the educational system, it is also naïve to imply that images in the media have absolutely no effect on the minds and priorities of our children and those who influence them.

Nor are the media entirely responsible for sending the right or wrong messages. The adults in the child's life, parents, teachers, counselors, coaches, professors, family members, and the public play an even greater role.

Let me share my own personal example: I grew up in India and spent 25 years there before I came to America in 1973. My father earned Rs. 500 a month. At today's rates, that would be about $11 a month for a family of three. Even adjusting for inflation, exchange rates, and comparative costs of living, by U.S. standards, our family income would be below the poverty line. I have no recollection of any "cool stuff" in my childhood. Sometimes, even school uniforms were hand-me-downs. But, here's the kicker: Even at that level of income, in all the years I lived at home, *there was never even one conversation, never one question as to <u>whether</u> I would go to college and graduate from college*. It was not a topic for discussion. *Not once.*

No matter what untold sacrifice it took on my parents' part or on mine, no matter how much hard work it entailed, and no matter how many "cool" things I would do without, I was going to college and was going to graduate from college.

My mother and father sent the right messages.

Today, I am in my 12th year as president of an excellent American university and I owe it to my parents, their values, and their messages of hard work and perseverance.

I was eligible to apply for the IIT after my first year of college as a Science (Math-Physics-Chemistry) major. About *four years* before I could even send in an application, my father clipped the IIT entrance exam advertisement from the newspaper and carried it around to show me from time to time! When it grew closer to the time I could apply, the IIT entrance examinations started to dominate my existence. For example, even in the summer "vacation," I got up early each day, went to an IIT entrance prep class, studied hard the rest of the day for the frequent tests given by the prep class, and did the same the next day—six days every week.

And, as hard as it was for me to get into IIT, it was even harder to graduate—competing with some of the best brains in the country. At the end of a grueling five-year education process (now reduced to four years), the graduates of these IITs earn the best engineering jobs in the country—now, with the flatter world, perhaps some of the best engineering jobs in the world.

Of course, there was parental pressure and years of hard work.

Is parental pressure a bad thing? I do not think so. I did not want to go to IIT—I went because of parental pressure. Today, I thank my parents—repeatedly—for that pressure and that decision. When I went to IIT, I was about 18. My parents were in their 50s. Is it unreasonable to expect that "Father and Mother (with a combined experience base of in excess of 100 years) know Best?" Why do we, in America, assume that the quality of decision-making at 18 (or younger) is superior to the knowledge base and rationality of parents in their 40s or 50s? Junior executives in industry defer to senior ones with more experience. Should not decisions that determine the course of one's life be advised by the experience base that exists in the family and the (older) adult environment?

Is hard work a bad thing? I do not think so. They were periods during my years at IIT that I would drop off to sleep out of sheer exhaustion. Red and bleary eyes are not the end of the world. Those work habits serve me in good stead even today. Besides, we need to understand that people in China and India, and in other parts of the world, are used to hard work. They are hungry and eager—for American jobs and American business. If we are to compete, we, too, need to be well used to hard work.

I believe we are sending the wrong messages to our kids. We should be working full time on an alternative definition of "cool." What is cool is not the cars they drive and the clothes they wear and the cell phones they have.

What is cool is having choices later in life, the ability to learn, and the ability to have an "untouchable" career in our rapidly changing world.

Many readers, when they read of my recommendations in favor of much more hard work, in favor of the benefits respecting the experience of parents, parental pressure, and the "Father and Mother know Best" phenomenon, in favor of postponed rather than instant gratification, will associate these values with *Asian* culture and claim that they have no place in America. If so, consider this: if you have an 85-year old or a 90-year old person in your family, ask him or her what life was like in America in the 1930s and 1940s. I suspect that they will say that these were all *American* values and strengths.

But why look back to a time long gone, while this entire article has been devoted to looking forward? One reason is that those were the days when America built the nation that rose to a leadership position in the world. Another reason is that the traditional American values of the 1930s and the 1940s are not globally outdated—they are what the competition is using, *today!*

There is a battle for the hearts and minds of young people. Images and stories help determine what is cool and what is not. If we choose the status quo and refuse to glorify academic accomplishments as fervently as we promote athletics, then we really cannot complain when the inevitable stories appear about American kids' poor academic performance.

ETHICS IN COLLEGE ATHLETICS

Our society knows that academic institutions often cut corners when it comes to athletes and athletics. Even a quick Internet search reveals numerous examples of "academic fraud," "unethical conduct," and "extra benefits" to student athletes. From awarding A's to students who never attend a class, to changing grades, to recalculating grade-point averages, to providing answer keys prior to an exam, some athletics programs have clearly placed athletic competition above academic achievement. In my favorite worst-case story, athletes were given a final exam comprised of multiple-choice questions such as, "How many points does a 3-point field goal account for in a basketball game?" or "How many goals are on a basketball court?" In this specific case, the coach's contract was not renewed, but it raises the question as to how many other examples of academic malfeasance exist in America's colleges and universities. Although I make no excuse for coaches who cut corners to give athletes an edge, it is equally scandalous that some university administrators, university supporters, and society wink at such practices. I applaud Miles Brand, President of the National Collegiate Athletics Association (NCAA), for his leadership in instituting comprehensive academic reform package for NCAA athletics. In word and in practice, I support the NCAA's efforts to ensure the academic success of its student athletes.

Contrast the academic shenanigans above with the statement in the Appendix, given in writing to UWG's Director of Athletics (AD) for wide distribution to his staff, which places student safety, academic success, and participation significantly ahead of winning games.

It is in writing. The coaches have it. And, it works. A brief anecdote might help. Cheerleading is a big deal at UWG—having won five consecutive national titles. On the way to a competition a year or so ago, the cheerleaders were headed into serious weather conditions. The Athletics Director called them and instructed them to turn around and come home. He then called me to ask whether I approved of his decision. My response: "Of course." End of discussion—have a nice day!

These things are not difficult.

As another example, during the past year when hurricanes hit the United States hard and resulted in gas shortages and very significant increases in utility costs, officials in many states insisted on restraint and cost-cutting measures in government agencies, including state universities. In some cases, professional development trips for faculty and staff were called off; in others, even those presenting papers at conferences or were otherwise on the program could not travel. This was disappointing, but many accepted it as being the unfortunate result of natural and economic disasters.

Question: How many football games were cancelled? Is there any ethical dilemma in telling faculty colleagues that they cannot travel because conferences represent nonessential trips, but that there will be no decrease of athletics travel?

Where are our priorities?

ACADEMIC FREEDOM AND THE COUNTER PRESSURES

I mentioned earlier that Friedman listed American colleges and universities as his number one "secret of American sauce." Another "secret of American sauce" he lists is the openness of our society. I agree. This is a very American characteristic. It needs to be cherished, nurtured, and protected. American colleges and universities have a special role to play here given our traditions of academic freedom.

"I may disapprove of what you have to say, but I shall defend to the death your right to say it." Voltaire.

There are challenges to free speech from outside the Academy *and from within*. A detailed treatment of these issues would require an entire article of its own. Here, I will simply say that we need some serious conversation about the topic. Lee Bollinger, President of Columbia University, in his remarks at the 2005 commencement exercises said:

> In journalism and politics, the emphasis used to be on reaching the largest and most diverse audience possible. That's one reason it's called 'broadcasting.' Today, though, it's a different story. The emphasis is on what some call 'narrowcasting.'
>
> Some politicians seem more concerned with 'solidifying their base' than building a bigger one. Many news organizations have become expert niche marketers: your views are categorized and catered to at every possible juncture. Meanwhile, think tanks and policy institutes are proliferating, each advancing particular ideologies.
>
> It's easy in this polarized climate to pick a side and become cloistered in one worldview, to the exclusion of all others. You listen to left-wing or right-wing talk radio—not both. You buy a book on Amazon and it instantly suggests five books just like it: the interest is not in broadening your tastes, but in reinforcing them. You can go through each day reading the newspaper, watching TV news, and surfing the Web—feeling highly informed of world events—and never encounter a view that's different from your own. [11]

That, as you know, is not how it works here.

While President Bollinger meant Columbia University when he said "here," for the purpose of this essay we may interpret "here" to mean higher education.

I do not suggest, nor does Bollinger, that we should abandon our beliefs. I do not suggest that there should be no responsibility for speech. However, when problems or grievances occur, I do believe that we (students, faculty, administrators, alike) should use *established university procedures* to process the grievance. If the speech is protected but offensive (and offensive speech is indeed protected by our laws), those views can be—if necessary—repudiated.

The American Association of University Professors' statement[12] on Academic Freedom and that of the Association of American Colleges and Universities provide us with good guidance through these difficult waters.[13]

Without pretending to bring this discussion to closure, I will say that, if we lose or reduce the ability to have civil discourse without being uncivil, to disagree without being disagreeable, or to ask questions and have "uncomfortable conversations," we will lose an important "secret of American sauce" and a crucial ingredient of academic life.

So . . . *Can* Universities Lead? Can *Universities* Lead? Can Universities *Lead*?

Yes; we can—if we are prepared to ask and answer the tough questions—not just of society but of ourselves. We cannot claim the right to question the very existence of God and yet not be willing or able to question the ingredients of a course, or of a successful candidacy (for recruitment, tenure, or promotion), or of the structure of an academic department.

And, how can universities provide ethical leadership in a global society? Through our traditional missions of Teaching, Scholarship & Research, and Service:

1. Education to help our children become increasingly prepared for the future, and to help the people of the world open their eyes to developmental opportunities rather than conflict;
2. Research and development to help with the problem of resource management and economic integration;
3. Helping people, communities, societies, states, and nations be in a position to receive some of the benefits of the 21st century.

We in higher education are uniquely situated to provide ethical leadership in a global society. Let us embrace that duty, that challenge, and that responsibility. It will not be easy, and we will not be able to do it alone. We need the help of our neighbors, our society, our friends, our funding partners, our spiritual leaders, the children of the world, and of their parents. As Winston Churchill said in his famous speech, *Blood, Toil, Tears, and Sweat*, "At this time I feel entitled to claim the aid of all, and I say, 'come then, let us go forward together with our united strength.'"

Note: The author is a Professor at, and President of, the University of West Georgia, but this piece is written in the author's private capacity and does not represent the views of any institution to which he belongs.

APPENDIX A

"THE SEARCH FOR PEACE AND HUMILITY"[14]

Today's world is very difficult to understand.

All over the world, we have several leaders—defined as those with significant followings—who claim to receive their commands directly from God.

And, each of them believes that that God wants them to wreak havoc on others so that *his* God's will is done (the male pronoun, unfortunately for this male writer, does not simply represent sexist use of the pronoun).

And, each of them believes that *his* God can whip everyone else's God, and that his vision of the world is the *only* one that can and should prevail.

And, none of them has the strength and the humility to question that *perhaps*, just perhaps, he is wrong.

And, each of them believes that war, rather than peace, is the answer.

And, each of them believes that the means—ranging from selective quoting and interpretation of scriptures, data and events, to bloodshed—justifies the end.

And, each of them is offended if anyone points out the similarity of his argument with those of his sworn enemy.

And, interestingly, each of them gains strength from the other; each is regarded more highly by his followers *because* of the actions of the other; and each of them is effectively a "campaign manager" for the others, *enhancing the popularity of his sworn enemy* within his own constituency.

And, unfortunately, each of them has followers who blindly follow the leader, believe as the leader tells them, rush to do the leader's bidding, and put themselves in harm's way, while the leaders sit in safety and plan and watch the mayhem (each one knowing, of course, that God personally gave him the right to send others to their deaths).

And, in creating this mayhem, each one of them is actually spending scarce resources that could be used to better the lives of his own people, thus *making his own people worse off.*

And, as all this mayhem is going on, no one—among the leaders or the followers—has the humility to wonder what the impact of these actions is on the world, the enemy, and his own people.

And, while it is *possible* that one of them is right (indeed, each of them sincerely believes that he is the one who is right), it is also possible that all of them are wrong, and that peace *is* the way to go.

And, while many of us just *know* that our leader is right, and that every opposing leader is wrong, let us have the awareness to recognize that there is similar conviction regarding another leader.

And, while most people want and crave for peace and humanity, the warmongers among us—leaders and followers both—are driving the world's agenda.

Today's world is very difficult to understand.

APPENDIX B

The University of West Georgia

Objectives and Priorities for Athletics

There are specific and critical objectives for the Director of Athletics and the Athletics staff, each of which must be met under the overarching umbrella of:

1. Sound ethical behavior and standards of the highest order, which includes compliance with NCAA and Conference rules and regulations; and
2. Sound fiscal prudence and appropriate management of the Athletics budget.

In order, these objectives are:

1. Safety;
2. Success of student athletes in terms of academics, retention, and graduation rates;
3. Opportunities for student athletes who have the necessary ability and commitment to develop and demonstrate their athletic abilities, with particular emphasis on Title IX issues; and
4. Spirit: the engendering of team and school spirit among players, the student body, and other supporters—which includes winning games.

The above are listed in decreasing order of importance. For example, rewards and sanctions will be dependent on all of the above, but *much more so* on student safety and academic success than on just the win–loss record.

CHAPTER 10

Cross-Sector Collaboration in the Public Interest

David J. Siegel and Michael J. Siegel

There was a time, either in actual fact or in the popular imagination, when classes of organizations had reliably differentiated "personalities" and could be counted on to conform more or less to the metaphors used to describe them. Corporations, for example, were profit machines. Government was a sprawling bureaucracy marked by red tape. The most persistent and enduring image of the academy was the "ivory tower," with its connotations of fortress-like insularity and a calculated remove from society. The use of the past tense is intentional, for the features encoded in such monikers have largely become relics of a bygone era. Today, these depictions seem mere caricatures—limited, distorted, and increasingly inaccurate. The modern condition is a boundaryless one that has obscured and complicated traditional notions of the roles universities, corporations, government organizations, and others play in the world, both on their own and in league with others. Etzkowitz and Leydesdorff[1] have even proposed the imagery of the "triple helix" to capture the braided quality of academic-industry-government relationships.

But even that expansive rendering fails to fully appreciate the dynamic web of interconnections that includes additional entities like nongovernmental organizations (NGOs), private foundations, nonprofits, community-based organizations, education providers, agencies, and associations. Alliances among and between these groups have become pervasive. Whether due to our nomadic impulses, the wish to expand our dominion, or the simple fact that the opportunities and interests pursued by organizations refuse to stay at home, something like a cross-boundary migration has ensued. The resultant linkages—and the transformations they engender—have been predictably tumultuous; partners chafe at the compromises required to live together peaceably and productively, even as they benefit immeasurably from interactions with their counterparts.

The central idea to be developed in this chapter is that social actors (colleges and universities primary among them) pursue an expanding array of activities in collaboration, which complicates conventional understandings of place and purpose. Using the higher education enterprise as our fulcrum, we attempt to (1) identify key aspects and examples of the changing landscape for multisector collaborations, (2) address some of the prominent challenges and considerations attendant in this model, (3) discuss the changing role of leadership and leaders in this evolving regime, and (4) outline a way forward, including questions to be asked and further possibilities to be explored.

THE CONTEXT FOR COLLABORATION

A View of the Landscape

The world at the beginning of the 21st century is flat,[2] linked,[3] networked,[4] a veritable global village whose many access points are within startlingly easy reach. These descriptors indicate properties of interdependence, complexity, convergence, cosmopolitanism, and connectedness—certainly nothing new under the sun. What has changed is the speed with which information, ideas, and cultural capital travel the globe, as well as the capacity of organizations to tackle problems of enlarged scope. Enabled by powerful tools and technologies, and emboldened by a sense of shared responsibility, social actors are finding that conditions are fertile for the formation and growth of collaborative ventures. What is more, alliances are virtually demanded as the only legitimate adaptive response to the considerable challenges in global health, human rights, education, economic development, and related spheres. Wider environmental currents of change, meanwhile, have been accompanied by fractal-like modifications *within* sectors.

The higher education setting, for example, has undergone profound (and interrelated) changes in recent years, including a growing emphasis on marketing and commercialization[5], a more direct role in technology transfer, an acceleration in privatization, the rise of academic entrepreneurship, and the emergence of a knowledge industry that extends far beyond the precincts of higher education and encompasses an array of content providers, competitors, and online and for-profit entities. The research university is more market-like in its behavior than ever before.[6] With closer formal ties between academe and the private sector has come a structural elaboration of offices and activities to facilitate technology licensing and transfer, protect the intellectual property of inventors, and manage the financial interests of institutions. Complex interactions among institutions have also evolved new organizational forms, including science parks, research hubs, and for-profit subsidiaries.[7] One of the concerns voiced by academics is that along with new opportunities for growth, the very culture of academe (not just its structure) is changing beyond recognition. (More about this later.) Whether one is inclined to cheer these developments for their possibilities or lament them as examples of traditional higher education's diminishing market share, there are long-term implications of this arrangement that we have only begun to think about.

As revolutionary as the changes have been in the postsecondary education sector over the last several years, they are perhaps no more unsettling than the ones experienced by the private sector. Here, notions like inclusive capitalism and corporate social responsibility, with their particular alchemy of social consciousness and profit maximization, have achieved the status of strategic imperatives. Environmental and social sustainability are increasingly viewed as core (not peripheral) preoccupations, contributing to an enlarged conception of the uses of the corporation.[8] Cross-sector ties involving universities, multinational corporations and their subsidiaries, government agencies, nongovernmental organizations, philanthropic organizations, and even grassroots activists are becoming more common in this space. Prahalad[9] views the very framework of world economic development and social transformation as a collaborative and tightly interconnected endeavor undertaken by private enterprise, development and aid agencies, local governments, civil society organizations, and entrepreneurs. Examples of cooperative problem solving in the developing world bear this out; a study by Brown[10] revealed that the mobilization and coordination of grassroots activists, government agencies, ministries, and NGOs played a key role in an immunization program in Bangladesh, an irrigation program in Indonesia, an urban sanitation program in Pakistan, and a savings development movement in Zimbabwe.

Forces Stimulating Collaboration

Of the major forces catalyzing cross-sector collaborations, financial pressures, and incentives are perhaps the most straightforward. On the higher education front, financial support from public sources makes up a dwindling percentage of the total funding mix.[11] Increasingly, state and federal revenues are being replaced by private dollars from corporations, foundations, wealthy alumni, endowment, and tuition. In some cases, particular academic units (schools and departments) within public universities are completely privatized.[12] The cultivation of external partnerships, then, becomes a pragmatic solution to resource constraints.

Research universities are also encountering calls for a more direct role in local, regional, national, and global economic development. Escalating demands and expectations for civic engagement, outreach, and other forms of interaction with its many publics—often at the behest of state lawmakers—are challenging all of higher education to behave more entrepreneurially. At the same time, there is a heightened awareness of the systemic nature of the major social challenges of our time, and enhanced cooperation between academic and industrial sectors is viewed as a matter of social obligation.[13] Public policy, most notably the Bayh–Dole Act of 1980, has also played an important role in encouraging universities to pursue commercialization opportunities by licensing their intellectual property (in the case of Bayh—Dole, inventions resulting from federally funded research) to the private sector for commercial development in the public interest. The National Science Foundation is among the bodies that have encouraged cross-sector partnerships to facilitate technological innovation in the United States. This same strategy has been applied in Europe, Asia, and Australia.[14]

The Benefits that Accrue

The picture that emerges is one in which expectations for the public interest role organizations should play in the world are expanding far beyond the internal capacities of these organizations, leading them to seek alliances that add complementary strengths and fresh approaches in key domains. Collaboration, after all, is an acknowledgment of the basic fact that no one organization or class of organizations on its own has the resources, connections, expertise, or intellectual capital to solve intractable problems or seize emerging opportunities. References to the collaborative advantage[15] and the alliance advantage[16] call attention to the immediate and long-term value that is created in partnership. Value can take the form of learning and special understandings, cooperative problem solving, and cross-boundary flows that include money, people, ideas, practices, energy, attitudes, and a host of other tangible and intangible assets.[17] A strategy and philosophy of collaboration, then, is a means of tapping into specialized knowledge, networks, and capabilities that are useful for project-related purposes but can also be used to nurture a larger feeling of social trust among partners.

Examples

Collaborations across sector lines take on several different forms, are predicated on many logics, display varying degrees of formality and coordination, and aim toward a range of outcomes. Strategic research alliances and joint ventures, for example, operate by different sets of rules and standards than, say, collaborative arrangements that have advocacy or talent development—rather than profitability—as their chief objective. Most of the literature dealing with academic–industry partnerships clearly gives pride of place to science-based research relationships, such as the high-profile one between UC-Berkeley and Swiss pharmaceutical giant Novartis. This amounts to a shortcoming in the body of knowledge on other kinds of collaborations, especially those with a social policy agenda. Two prime examples help to illustrate the effective use of collective action and partnership in the social arena.

The first example (and the one representing the broadest spectrum of intersector coalition building) comes from the recent legal challenge to the use of race as a factor in collegiate admissions. In 2003, when two lawsuits brought against the University of Michigan (*Gratz versus Bollinger* and *Grutter versus Bollinger*) made their way to the U.S. Supreme Court, a remarkable cross-section of organizations and individuals submitted amicus briefs supporting the consideration of race in admissions decisions. The roster of advocates included many prominent Fortune 500 companies, military leaders, professional associations like the American Psychological Association, groups like the National Urban League and the American Jewish Committee, numerous colleges and universities, members of congress, senators, individual states, and human rights organizations, to name just a few. The amicus briefs singly and collectively made the case that successful efforts to improve minority representation in professional life depend heavily on the flow of underrepresented students through the nation's institutions of higher education. Members of the Fortune 500, for example, argued that the diversification of senior management ranks and corporate boards, which is important for business reasons, is significantly aided by the development of a diverse pool of talent in colleges and universities. Using similar rationales, the various sectors formed a powerful social compact to democratize education and open new pathways of access and opportunity for minority students.

This principle is brought into sharper view in the second example. To deepen the pool of qualified minority students in critical areas like science, math, engineering, and business, many companies and nonprofit organizations

126

FOR THE COMMON GOOD

(including major private foundations) are partnering with academic institutions to create long-range pipeline development initiatives. The leadership education and development (LEAD) program in business is one such venture. LEAD is a partnership of twelve top American business schools, nearly forty leading multinational corporations, and a nonprofit umbrella organization that plays a central coordinating role. In LEAD, companies not only provide financial support but play a crucial role in program design and delivery, effectively functioning as public educators. (Arguably, what is initiated in a highly integrated multisector collaboration of this type is a form of role hybridization.) Pipeline development programs such as LEAD represent an important public–private partnership that simultaneously serves organizational self-interest and wider public interest.

CHALLENGES AND CONSIDERATIONS

Collaborations, of course, are not all sweetness and light. Broadly, they have been viewed in terms of (1) a deficit model in which external alliances are held to dilute the integrity of focal organizations and (2) an additive model in which something new and powerful gets created in the mix.

From the vantage point of higher education, there are several questions raised by closer ties among sectors, specifically in the realm of academic–industry relationships. For example, what is the role of the arts and humanities in partnership arrangements that, for the moment, are clearly favoring the sciences, business, and engineering? What does the growing disparity between "haves" and "have-nots" among the disciplines mean for the long-term vitality of institutions of higher education? Do our campuses risk becoming mere R&D labs to corporate America, so that noncommercial knowledge or discoveries are devalued? Are we creating a new class system among postsecondary institutions based on commercial value and prospects, with resources simply enriching the already rich and impoverishing those without connections (a classic case of "the lion's share going to the lion")? How might partnerships—with their promise of resources and connections—indirectly or directly reorder the balance of power within the academy? How do students benefit from the commercial activity or ambitions of university researchers or programs? Do partnerships result in efforts by companies to bend academic policy to corporate aims and objectives, as some critics have alleged? Does collaboration help or hinder our efforts to better serve the public interest? How can partnerships with the nonprofit community and the private sector better serve educational, economic development, and public interest aims? Will external partners come to be the ultimate judge of the value and uses of higher education? These questions contain elements of conflicts of interest, conflicts of commitment, and conflicts of values.

Culture Clash

Nearly five decades ago, C.P. Snow called attention to the gap between the cultures of science and the humanities.[18] This gulf between the two cultures has widened on campuses in recent years with the infusion of cash to support commercially viable scientific research. A broader culture clash, though, is the one between the competing value systems of academe and industry. This dichotomy has been represented as "freedom of inquiry, the open sharing of knowledge, a commitment to rigorous study, and a love of learning" that are the hallmark of universities, in contradistinction to the "return on investment and shareholder value" that is the focus of corporations.[19] Critics of relational ties between the two sectors warn of the threats to academic freedom and academic culture more generally when commercialization enters the calculus.[20] Some have gone so far as to allege that corporate influence is corrupting higher education.[21] Worries about the loss of autonomy or the onset of a pernicious form of cultural hegemony are inevitable by-products of collaboration. Will we have to look and act more like our partners in order to get along effectively and efficiently? Will we be able to play the historically valued role of dispassionate social critic, even when doing so potentially jeopardizes critical funding relationships?

Much of the analysis of higher education in an age of money (to use the phrasing of Engell and Dangerfield[22]) tends to excoriate universities for making Faustian bargains with corporate patrons. To be fair, though, a good deal of the suspicion about closer ties among sectors appears to be built on the traps of monolithic thinking, the tendency to view prospective partners not on their own merits and attributes but on those ascribed to the whole class of organizations of which they are a part, so that wholesale evaluations are substituted for case-by-case assessments of the suitability of prospective partners. Clearly, this lack of specificity and particularity can diminish the appetite for collaboration and lead opponents to claim prima facie incompatibility before the due diligence is done. Moreover, partners are often in conflict not over core values but over more pedestrian issues such as time horizons for the completion of joint projects. The quarterly earnings targets that are a fixture of corporate culture have no real analogue in academic life, where the gestation period for new ideas and inventions is much longer. In the scheme of things, these practical matters are much more navigable than philosophical concerns or questions of ethics.

A Question of Integrity?

The ethical issues raised by collaboration are manifold but may be viewed as emanating from a single overarching concern: How can alliances proceed in a way that preserves the distinctive qualities and core values—the ethos—of colleges and universities (and those of partnering organizations)? Indeed, one of the principal concerns about cross-sector collaborations appears to be on the grounds that they pollute the purity of institutional forms, an argument that has been explored on the cross-cultural level by Appiah.[23] The blurring and blending of role expectations suggests innovative possibilities, but hybridization can also be terribly disorienting. Further, such developing alliances can be equally threatening to the respective partnering organizations as well as public in general. To be sure, the American public's almost trigger-like disdain for questionable ethical practices in many areas of government, business and industry, education, and other sectors almost ensures that any such partnerships will endure a significant amount of scrutiny in all stages of development and implementation.

There is no question that as activities and missions have radiated outward, they have resulted in adjacencies and overlaps where organizations have become virtually indistinguishable in key elements of form and function. Consider that there are corporate universities and university corporations, an amusing example of such convergence. Those who argue for differentiation—and the integrity of differentiation—essentially make the claim that it is, after all, an important ecological consideration. Seen from this angle, the functional differentiation of organizations or sectors is necessary for the effective functioning of the whole system, and efforts to maneuver outside of one's area of specialization can be disruptive to the maintenance of a delicate environmental balance.[24]

The Concentric Circles of Collaboration

Partnerships are always enmeshed in a net of strong and weak ties; relations among parties cannot be understood without also recognizing the *additional* webs of alliances in which each of the partners is suspended.[25] Plainly, this complex arrangement dramatically increases the likelihood that a collaboration will be affected in some way by the actions of distantly and indirectly related agents somewhere on the grid (but off of the radar). If institutions are judged by the company they keep, what happens when our partners (or the partners of our partners) engage in improprieties—legal, ethical, or otherwise? Do we risk being painted with the same brush, and how do we monitor and manage potential problems along these lines? One of the costs we bear in a collaboration matrix is that greater attention must be paid to the indirect and unintended effects of activities undertaken by alliance members. If we are not keenly aware of the impacts of our counterparts' behavior and decisions in the world, we potentially compromise our own ethical standards. This is an exhausting proposition but one that may be made easier—not harder—by the multiplication of interdependencies. Collaborations, after all, extend the boundary spanning capabilities of organizations and can enable them to better anticipate such potentialities.

Stakeholders—interest groups that feel entitled or empowered to make claims on organizational governance or outputs—play an increasingly important role in this arrangement. The ranks of normative stakeholders (those owed an obligation) and derivative stakeholders (those able to influence organizational decisions or actions)[26] have proliferated in and across all sectors, a fact that necessitates greater sensitivity to monitoring and satisfying their expectations. One of the effects of porous boundaries is that many more groups are able to shape organizational policy and hold organizations accountable for ethical conduct. For example, several universities have divested from companies doing business in Sudan, where thousands have been killed in government-supported genocide in the Darfur region. Campus chapters of Students Taking Action Now: Darfur (STAND) have been instrumental in lobbying administrators at Stanford, Harvard, Yale, Dartmouth, Brown, and Amherst for the decision.[27] Examples like this point to the vast, distributed, and diffuse network of overseers who use their positions—and the viral power of social capital—to agitate and advocate for change. Clearly, it is a power that is multiplied through intersector linkages.

Reframing Collaboration as a Citizenship Opportunity

Concerns about cultural divides and protecting the integrity of institutional forms can often have the effect of sidestepping the larger issue of how the public interest might be better served by the collective resources of sectors working together. As James Freedman, former president of Dartmouth, has observed, universities are prone to be "self-serving when they ought to be altruistic . . . self-absorbed when they ought to be socially committed."[28] The same might be said of other institutional types. Freedman's admonition applies with equal force to all sectors; they must view themselves as embedded in a wider social context and system in which their actions have consequences for every other inhabitant of the system. This, of course, requires an acute sense and awareness of wholeness—a peripheral, macroscopic, multidimensional view of the landscape. By viewing collaborations in terms of the benefits that redound to publics and stakeholders, rather than as empire-building opportunities for the organizations themselves, much good can come of cross-sector alliances.

ACADEMIC LEADERSHIP: PROBLEMS AND PROMISES

America witnessed at the turn of the 20th century an emerging specialization in nearly all academic disciplines, which ultimately led to the balkanization of many colleges and universities into a loose collective of departments and programs whose loyalties were directed more to the profession at large than to the institutions in which they were housed. Meanwhile, there was a seismic shift in focus from liberal education to a more practical education that would address burgeoning industrial priorities. These interlaced developments have had significant consequences: they have helped fuel the rise of a highly diversified system of education that makes it possible (and prudent) for colleges and universities to engage in collaborative arrangements with external constituents, but they also produced the conditions of fragmentation that present special challenges to leaders of academic enterprises. Today, a heavily decentralized organizational structure and the rewards associated with entrepreneurial free-agency are salubrious to the pursuit of cross-sector partnerships, even as they make it more difficult for leaders to manage the partnership process.

Decentralization

Institutions of higher education are exceedingly complex and comprehensive organizations that house an astonishing variety of fields of study, scholarly interests, and administrative offices. Each of the academic disciplines, units, and functional areas operates as a largely autonomous community in its own right, resulting in the fabled ghettos and silos that have subdivided the city of intellect. Naturally, such milieus must be governed or led with a great deal of finesse, savvy, and subtlety. As higher education has moved (or stumbled) toward tighter coupling with the outside world, with independent fiefdoms opportunistically pursuing relevant external relationships, it has called into question the role of centralized leadership in facilitating or promoting *institutional* partnerships.

The unevenness with which campus units court and benefit from external collaborations, of course, reflects and reproduces patterns of difference among disciplines. This incongruity is not necessarily a problem to be solved; the more troubling phenomenon would be for disparities to persist out of sheer ignorance of collaborative possibilities or a lack of access to procedural knowledge and networks. To the extent that some fields or functional areas corner the market on collaborations with desirable entities (such as major funding sources) and erect barriers to entry for their peers across campus, a policy of equal opportunity may need to be enforced and coordinated by centralized leadership.

ACADEMIC ENTREPRENEURSHIP

It is tempting for some to believe that collaborative arrangements are foisted on the academy or grow out of conditions of privation that simply necessitate external support. Far from being merely the passive recipients of these sorts of pressures, though, academics are often remarkably self-motivated to locate and nurture relationships that will help translate their idea capital into some socially useful product, service, or venture. So it is that individual faculty members, not necessarily whole units or departments, are often the ones in the vanguard with respect to forging closer ties with industry, community-based organizations, government agencies, and others. The sense of free agency with which they pursue their scholarly agendas sometimes carries over into the initiation of collaborations, leading campus leaders to wonder how such discrete activity might be harnessed for the good of the whole institution. How, in other words, can instances of faculty entrepreneurship and unit-driven collaboration connect up to synergistically yield something greater than the sum of its parts? How is the learning from such partnerships to be captured and shared? How is value to be extracted and leveraged so that collaboration itself becomes an institutional core competency? How might the learning be used to improve performance, act as an informal monitoring mechanism, or serve as an accountability check?

The net effect of individual and unit-driven collaborations—combined with the ubiquity of stakeholders insinuating themselves into institutional decision-making—is a further flattening or democratization of leadership. In this realm, leadership emerges much more from grass roots, with many more visionary ideas coming from activists, agitators, pressure groups, interest groups, coalitions, internal units and departments, and individuals—and the powers of mobilization to bring them to fruition.

How, then, should universities manage the vast and sprawling network of often marginally coupled collaborative arrangements, along with the internal cultural divides that result? To what extent should institutions serve as the progenitors and incubators of partnerships, rather than accepting them as they come along? What might be done, to enroll or enfranchise more (and different) disciplines in the partnership process, so that areas like the arts and humanities are included in the mix along with the sciences? Fostering a culture and climate of interdisciplinary sharing, so that faculty in various quarters of the campus can tap into the stores of experience that are resident in their midst, is something that campus leaders are in a position to encourage and support. This is at heart an issue of institutional learning. Examples abound in the interdisciplinary efforts of several research universities to introduce scientists to the business aspects of commercializing their inventions and discoveries, a process that both teaches and models the power of collaboration. But in the search for interdisciplinary and cross-sector relationship building, what are the ethical implications for leadership?

Ethical Considerations of Cross-Sector Collaboration

Higher education leaders, like leaders in other sectors, typically consider a multiplicity of ramifications when making decisions. They are primarily concerned with the impact their decisions will have on the financial, legal, cultural, and psychological well-being of the institution, among other things. While a fundamental concern for the nature of ethical discourse is perhaps embedded in the decision-making process, it appears to be more implied than explicitly stated. Given several factors—the relatively cautious climate in academe, the financial state of many institutions, the nature of institutional branding and desire for mass market appeal—it is not surprising that some leaders may be more comfortable with addressing the legal, financial, pragmatic, and aesthetic implications of decisions made on campus than with the moral, ethical, and spiritual. And they may be better equipped to do so. As James Davis has suggested, "Conscientious administrators put forth sincere efforts to make decisions in a rational rather than arbitrary manner and they check these decisions for legal implications, but decisions can also be reviewed for their ethical ramifications."[29]

Perhaps testing a decision for its financial or legal implications is a simpler and less contentious process than, say, discerning the nature of its ethical dimensions. This is no consolation, however, given the ethically sensitive nature of decision-making in academe and the consequences of ascribing greater importance to practical and efficient standards than to moral and principled ones. Davis goes on to question, "What are the dimensions of a decision that can be called ethical and what help can be found in the field of ethics for testing a decision for its morality?"[30] The nontrivial point here is that leaders, for a variety of reasons, appear to be more adept (or perhaps just more comfortable) at addressing the legal and financial implications of institutional decisions, but seem more challenged in testing those same decisions for moral and ethical implications. Perhaps it is the failure of the academy to mandate ethics training—or at least require a course on ethics—in the preparation of students for professional and leadership roles in society. As Shapiro and Stefkovich[31] point out, we typically look to the professional schools—law, business, medicine, and the like—when discussing ethics in the curriculum, as they provide at least some type of required ethics-based component for their respective graduate students. But it is ironic that many schools of education— which not only train future teachers but also future administrative leaders— have no such requirement for their graduate students.

Ethical leadership has been explored extensively in the literature on education as well as field of organizational behavior.[32] Yet, there is a paucity of literature on leadership as it relates to collaborative work among leaders and organizations and the building of cross-sector or interdisciplinary alliances. Our purpose here is not to suggest an ethically grounded paradigm for collaborative leadership, though one is clearly needed. Rather, our intent is to describe some of the things leaders do when they collaborate and further encourage leaders to consider the ethical considerations of their work when they seek partnerships and generate alliance among industry, government, and other actors external to the college. David Chrislip and Carl Larson provide a useful look at the collaborative leadership process, essentially suggesting that collaborative leaders (1) inspire commitment and action, (2) lead as peer problem solvers, (3) build broad-based involvement, and (4) sustain hope and participation.[33] Among the more effective behaviors collaborative leaders employ include convening and energizing others; overcoming cynicism; relinquishing some element of control in the process; being inclusive of community and partner interests; sharing ownership; and relying on incremental goal attainment. To be sure, these are lofty behavioral goals to which a leaders should adhere in the process of cross-sector partnering. And the challenge to do so is that much more intensified when leaders must review and assess the efficacy of collaboration in light of ethical and moral implications.

A WAY FORWARD

An Education Agenda

There is a whole research and teaching agenda to be developed around the nature and conduct of cross-sector partnerships, an agenda that might draw on various social science research methods—such as the ethnographic techniques associated most closely with the field of anthropology—to understand the lived experiences of different sectors in interaction with each other. This could be done with an eye to understanding the full spectrum of interactions, their starting conditions, and how they take shape differently across various settings of interest. Data from such research could produce insights that would be potentially helpful for all parties. To the extent that much of current perception rests on misconceptions and misinformation, one way to ameliorate the problem would be to spend time exploring the phenomenon, perhaps with a prolonged sense of engagement, with the idea that it is far better to operate from a position of knowledge and experience.

In addition to putting collaboration under the microscope for research purposes, seeding the next generation of collaborators—that is, preparing students for a world of cross-sector interactions—is a critically important education function. Consider the power of the American Democracy Project, a national project developed by the American Association of State Colleges and Universities (AASCU) in collaboration with the New York Times, whose purpose it is to increase the civic awareness and engagement of students at AASCU-member institutions and foster a culture of civic responsibility among colleges and universities. At the time of this writing, more than 200 AASCU colleges and universities, representing more than 1.7 million students, are participating in the project. The particular role of *The New York Times*, the industry partner in this alliance, is not only to foster communication and assist with the dissemination of materials, opinion pieces, and campus success stories but to also advocate for change and encourage the exploration of contemporary issues related to citizenship and community.

Developing *institutional* appetite for collaboration is also important. A notable alliance along these lines is *Campus Compact*, a presidential organization that brings together more than 950 college and university presidents who are committed to framing, interpreting, and strengthening the civic purposes of the higher education system. The organization not only provides resources for fostering civic- and citizenship-related activities on college campuses, it provides advocacy and support as well as leadership opportunities. Embedded in the philosophy of this and other coalition organizations is that notion that citizenship and ethics are fundamentally intertwined.

Finally, many colleges and universities around the country actively promote and facilitate cooperative education, or co-op, programs, which are essentially organized to integrate classroom work with practical industry experience. Co-op programs are by their very design geared toward developing a symbiotic relationship with external partners in an effort to foster student learning as well as personal and professional growth and development. As a highly enriching—and mutually profitable—covenant between colleges and universities and business and industry, cooperative education represents a promising model for the development of cross-sector alliances between college and community entities that extend beyond the classroom.

Developing Deeper Understanding

As much as cross-sector partnerships are an essential and growing feature of the global landscape, it is surprising how little collaborators sometimes know about each other. This lack of knowledge and understanding breeds fear, loathing, and a perpetual state of suspicion. Many critics of academic-industry linkages think only of Enron and Tyco when they think of the corporation at all—they do not, for example, admit Whole Foods or Birkenstock (two environmentally and socially conscious organizations) into their conception of big business. They seem unaware that a corporate social responsibility revolution is underway, in which multinationals are busily working to be better stewards of the natural environment, better citizens of their communities, and more respectful of cultural diversity. This is a positively enlightened notion of the corporate role in the cosmos, and yet many in the academy still associate business almost exclusively with greed, degradation, and corruption. For their part, many in the business community still view academics as existing in a cloistered world far removed from the realities of everyday life. They see the academy as out of touch, unresponsive, existing for its own amusement rather than for any practical purpose, and concerned primarily with arcane matters. They do not tend to see the examples of academic capitalism and entrepreneurial activity that have become the norm on many campuses. Clearly, both camps harbor vague and outdated ideas about each other, which is ironic given that the educational pipeline is presumably closely connected to the other pipelines of, say, business, industry, government, and other sectors. That is, colleges and universities channel millions of students through the educational pipeline each year and feed thousands of corporations and other organizational entities waiting at the other end. A greater sense of mindfulness and attentiveness in the development of cross-sector collaborations—a conscientious attempt to know as we wish to be known—would benefit the process immeasurably and ultimately create a more symbiotic connection—literally and figuratively—among the vast maze of pipelines.

Partnerships can actually help sectors, organizations, and individuals update their views of each other, functioning as they do to create ports of entry into others' philosophies, practices, and even psyches. These linkages serve very specific purposes (research collaborations, for example, or helping to develop recruitment pipelines), but they also serve the more general purpose of creating zones of understanding and revelation. As partners seek to show good faith in joint ventures, something like a sympathetic imagination can develop that can be used for other purposes. A fund of good will and understanding, in other words, potentially gets developed in the process. Ultimately, it is the broader public that stands to gain the most from deeper and richer ties among sectors.

Global Ethical Leadership and Higher Education: "Being the Change You Wish to See"

Lawrence Edward Carter Sr.

The world of the 21st century requires an altogether new kind of leadership. The old attitudes and self-serving approaches of so many of today's leaders are not sufficient for our spirit-challenging times. But how will we develop a generation of ethically grounded leaders who are committed to the *common* good of humanity?

Many of us are hopeful that "the world is on the cusp of a new spirituality" with the potential to unify humanity[1]. And if this is ultimately realized, it will be credited in large part to leaders in higher education—leaders who have succeeded in building a diversity-mature academy, full of "higher-order thinking skills"[2] resulting from effective teaching and solid learning. For the university, more than any other institution is uniquely positioned to lead the way.

This unifying thinking has been ushered to this point by drum majors like John Shelby Spong (with his affirmative use of sacred text), Joseph Campbell, Daisaku Ikeda, Neale Donald Walsch, Shirin Ebadi, Deepak Chopra, Ernest Holmes, Sri Sri Ravi Shankar, Martin Luther King Jr., Mahatma Gandhi, Sri Mata Amritanandamayi Devi's (Amma), the Dalai Lama, Andrew Cohen, Charles Filmore, J. Krishnamurti, Robert Maynard Hutchins, Howard Washington Thurman, Benjamin Elijah Mays, Betty L. Seigel, Daniel Y. Habuki, Charles S. Finch III, Derek Bok, Cornell West, and Harry R. Lewis.

These drum majors were, and are, spiritually aware visionary activists, whose legacies transcend their cultures, nationalities, races, faith traditions, liturgical and scholarly orthodoxy, and the dying definitions of fanaticism. The soulful excellence of leadership of these drum majors transcends civil law sanctioned by the state, religious law sanctioned by the church or God, natural law sanctioned by nature, and logical law sanctioned by intelligence, and instead rests squarely on ethical laws or principles sanctioned by rational will[3]. They have sought an enlightened solidarity for humanity.

Three global citizens from three different cultures and countries, who share a common path of profound dedication to spirituality and reconciliation, have been recognized internationally. They, I believe, over the last 100 years, have been the chief engineers on the rainbow bridge to the cusp of a new ethical spirituality arousing the world's social potential in the new century.

Mohandas "Mahatma" Gandhi's civil disobedience and nonviolent demonstrations won greater freedom and ultimately independence for 400 million citizens of India after three centuries of British rule. Martin Luther King Jr.'s nonviolent commitment to peace and justice inspired the American movement for civil and human rights, giving voice to the hopes and dreams of the dispossessed throughout the world.

Daisaku Ikeda's work as a leading Buddhist philosopher, author, educator, humanist, founder, and social activist has led to the nonviolent democratization of Japan's feudalistic social structures and an international grassroots initiative of intercultural, interfaith dialogue and educational cooperation for global peace.

Against the backdrop of these three ethically oriented pedagogical giants, I want to discuss the new unifying superpowers: *peace* and *nonviolence*, which are leading us to the cusp of a new academy, a new spirituality, a new conscious evolution, a new global civility, and a new ethically grounded reconciliation for humanity. We are standing at a new crossroads of life on earth. All of our anguishes, challenges, crises, difficulties, problems, and struggles are the result of divided knowledge. All of our solutions will be the result of unified knowledge—a pedagogy of reconciliation.

BECOMING THE CHANGE WE SEEK

Today there is a movement in business, education, physics, religion, and theology, and outside all of them, not to find out how we are different, but how we are similar. We recognize that there is only one river of wisdom, but many wells[4].

To grow spiritually I believe we have to stop quoting scripture, any sacred scripture, as evidence of our beliefs, and start looking for the deeper meaning that these sacred stories hold, what James W. Fowler calls "Universalizing Faith."[5]

Spiritual growth is often held back because of literal translations of sacred texts, which create stagnation. We must focus on the wisdom the great teachings have in common, the pattern that unites us across all boundaries. We can come from different backgrounds to initiate an evolving consciousness of active nonviolence and peace among youth and adults globally. The choices we make now will create the future with which not only we, but also our children, will have to live and die. We intend to give our children a world that is better than the one we have received; a world free from the strategies of deliberate failure; "a world not of weaponry, but of livingry"; a place in which our children may learn compassionate emotion, compassionate listening, empathetic communication, unconditional love, nonjudgmental justice—where they do not participate in negativity.[6]

However, you cannot have what you are not willing to be. If you want peace, you have to be peaceful. It was J. Krishnamurti who said, "What you are the world is, and without your transformation there can be no transformation of the world".[7] You cannot give away what you do not possess. You must be the ideal itself to transform the national presidencies and the political culture of prime ministries. Violence is like a disease; It affects everyone but has a way of hitting the youngest among us the hardest.

Over 100 million people died in the 20th century in war and violence. At the beginning of the 20th century, such deaths were predominately among soldiers. By the end of the century, 80 percent were civilians and, tragically, the majority of these were women and children.

Nobel Peace Prize laureate Betty Williams, of Northern Ireland, spoke at Morehouse College in 2003 and informed us that half the population of Iraq is less than 15 years of age. We must seek to vaccinate ourselves with an evolving nonviolent consciousness lest we become known as a generation of youth killers. We must live according to what is possible in the outcome. We must learn to live in the results for which we pray. We need a campaign equal to our capacity to love and to be creative. We must carry and act on the consciousness of peace like F.W. de Klerk of South Africa who did the right thing and saved South Africa from a blood bath. Governments cannot give us peace. We must give peace to one another, and we must start with our children, says Mahatma Gandhi.

Barbara Marx Hubbard informs us that there is a great shift going on and we are about to move in mass from *homo-sapien-sapien*, which simply means being conscious that we are conscious, to a next stage where we are able to love the whole and not just the parts. It is said that over 50 million people in the United States, and a much larger number worldwide, have crossed over from *homo-sapien-sapien* to *homo-universalis,* becoming universal humans, able to embrace the world.[8] That is what Gandhi, King, Ikeda, Shirin Ebadi, Mother Theresa, Michael Nobel, and Prince El Hassan Bin Talal of Jordan as architects of peace and reconciliation have done. Can you love the whole and not just the parts, or, are you only capable of loving the parts?

Gandhi, King, Ikeda, and Judge Ebadi believed that violence does matter. Is it possible that, at a personal level, the most lethally violent threat to evolutionary ethical and spiritual awareness may be our own addictions? Robert O. Young, the great-great grandson of Brigham Young, tells us that addiction is violence to oneself.[9] We see what happens in the world when we do not have what it takes to be human. If we are to properly see the ethical interconnectedness of the world, then we must eliminate our violence-producing addictions in order to discover how previously divided religious traditions are converging into a river of sacredness, interspirituality, and an awareness of "one humanity."

We have developed to this point at the end of 15 billion years of evolution. Michael Bernard Beckwith has said, when you fail or refuse to evolve or manifest the best that you know, God is stillborn in your life. It was George Bernard Shaw who said, "Better keep yourself clean and bright; you are the window through which you must see the world.[10] And William Wordsworth said, "Come forth into the light of things. Let nature be your teacher."[11]

Most readers will have heard the statement: You must "be the change you wish to see".[12] Be the change. Do not just preach it, practice it. Do not just dream it, live it. Be the thing itself. Do not give lip service, give life service. Do not politic over nonviolence, download it into your bio data.

GANDHI AND THE FIRST "9/11" EVENT

This quotation—"be the change"—gives us some idea of the ground upholding the principles of nonviolence. It is believed to have originated with Mahatma Gandhi in 1906, when the campaign for Indian rights began to take root among people in Johannesburg, South Africa, fulfilling the writings of Count Leo Tolstoy of Russia. The year was 1906; but are you aware of the date? On *September 11,* 1906 Gandhi conducted his first nonviolent campaign.[13] So now we have an alternative to how we may view "9-11." The occasion when the World Trade Center towers collapsed triggered the opening of the hearts of the people of the world so that, for the first time in modern history, the hearts of the world opened up to embrace the suffering. The tragedy is that our hearts did not stay open long.

Will it take this kind of trigger always to get us to realize that we are not separate on this planet, and that Martin Luther King Jr.'s words were indeed prophetic: "Injustice anywhere is a threat to justice everywhere?"[14]

Ikeda has founded two universities built on a pedagogy of peace. The first such university in the United States is in Orange County, California. He has institutionalized the evolutionary philosophies of nonviolence, peace, and spiritual awareness of Gandhi and King.[15]

We in higher education are called not to a new religion or to an ideology for overpowerment, but to Betty L. Siegel's concept of an "international alliance for invitational education" for empowerment.[16] It is a call to spiritual awareness, to ethically based leadership, to lives as global citizens, universal humans, and planetary incarnations. To achieve this route to professional and personal success, we must be trailblazers, not pathfinders. Our goal is to be transcultural, because separate cultures are not necessarily the friend of enlightenment.

Gandhi, King, Ikeda—an Indian Hindu, an African-American Christian, and a Japanese lay Buddhist—each acknowledged an American white man, Henry David Thoreau, a transcendentalist and 1837 graduate of Harvard University. They acknowledged him as the one who tutored them on civil disobedience and nonviolence, a method for dealing with unjust governments.

The best solutions and methods to our current planetary crisis have come to us through a cross-fertilization that literally belts the world. But you will never find these solutions and methods if you do not get out of the box: the age box, the race box, the gender box, the faith box, the nation box, the diet box, and the ideology box. An African Proverb from Central Uganda says: "He who never visits thinks his mother is the best cook."[17] The dates September 11, 2001, *and* September 11, 1906, are calls from the universe that we are not separate. In the case of Thoreau, his inspiration to be a transcendentalist was acquired from a French woman, Madame Germaine de Staël. She, in turn, was influenced by German philosophers.[18]

Likewise, stepping out of the box of male chauvinism and sexism, Gandhi frequently acknowledged that his wife, Kasturbai, taught him nonviolence. Gandhi began his career with a violent temperament. The fact that his wife was a good, unassuming Hindu woman is probably the reason most people were not aware of her effect on the Mahatma. But during the 10 years that Gandhi was in jail, his wife made his speeches, ate his nonviolent diet, and aroused women of India to get involved. It was the way she responded to his violent tendencies that changed the course of history.

Gandhi indicated that women have a natural predisposition for providing nonviolent leadership. Men give orders, but women bring order. Gandhi announced to the world that in order for him to free India, he had to become a woman. Personal power results from a balance of both masculine and feminine forces. The spiritualization process, in men as well as in women, is a feminization process, a quieting of the mind. Gandhi's acknowledgement is the cusp of an ancient ethical spirituality, remembered.

Gandhi, King, Ikeda, Ebadi, Thoreau, Holmes, The Filmores, Tolstoy, Nobel, De Klerk, Mandela, Mother Theresa, Beckwith, Jean Houston, Hubbard, and Prince Hassan defined their faith not by its boundaries, but by its roots. Do not limit your faith's manifestation by the name of your religion or denomination. There is not a scientific truth and a religious truth. The truth is truth worldwide. Our ignorance will become increasingly costly if we do not get out of our boxes.

September 11 is a call from the universe that we are not separate. Not everybody, however, can easily be a global citizen. The fact that America (which is 6 percent of the world's population) consumes 30 percent of the world's resources forces many non-Americans to focus on their limitations and not their possibilities. Can we so-called "first world citizens" be secure with most of the world at risk? Ikeda talks about the "interdependent co-arising of all things". American individualism is at an end. Globalization means interdependence. Our planet has become one whole. The Internet is our planetary nervous system. We are all changed by the choices, voices and visions of our neighbors. But we have a shortage of humanists.

America is engaged in a pluralist experiment. Chicago has 70 mosques, Atlanta has 30, and there are more American Muslims than there are American Episcopalians, Jews, and Presbyterians combined. Los Angeles is now the largest Buddhist city in the Western Hemisphere with over 300 temples. Chaplains of all faiths are now in the American military. The U.S. Navy opened its first mosque and commissioned its first Muslim chaplain in 1990. There is a certain epistemological arrogance about thinking we have found it all and circled our wagons around it.[19]

For 1,500 years we have heard the argument that we cannot deal with so much diversity. The ironies of this exclusion have produced histories of blood hatreds. We cannot insist that everyone look like us. We must engage the pluralism. The time of not knowing each other is over. The composite portrait of ourselves is coming into focus. Diversity is not excellence, it is just a fact that we must deal with. Pluralism is not diversity alone, but engagement; not a gift but an achievement; not tolerance, but seeking understanding. Our ignorance will be increasingly costly if we do not get out of our disciplinary neighborhoods or religious boxes. Pluralism requires the encounter of differences and coherent self-criticism, or coherent self-awareness.

What kind of person is required to awaken humanity to its spiritual magnificence? Or to awaken a higher-learning academy that is heart deep and worldwide and ethically grounded? Andrew Cohen, founder of *What Is Enlightenment?* magazine, points us toward an answer when he says, "What an alien concept the evolution of consciousness actually is in our culture. We are almost never encouraged to grapple with our own evolutionary potential . . ." And then he asks, "What would it be like to develop and grow at a level so profound that I would never be able to see it and yet others would be able to recognize its expression? If we can even begin to look deeply into this question, mysteriously we will already be participating in the very evolution of consciousness I 've been speaking about."[20]

Those who are cultivating a deep and wide sustainable symphony of values can more easily connect with others, and are participating in the consciousness about which Cohen speaks. Gandhi stood at the cusp of a new ethical spirituality, a new value creation. He showed that people in authority should be very careful how they deal with a person who has no need for sensual pleasure, for riches, for comfort or praise, or promotion, but is simply committed to doing what is right. Such people are dangerous enemies because their bodies, which can always be destroyed, give others so little power upon their souls.

What needs to happen that would allow more people to take a quantum jump to a place to build a world of peace, reconciliation, and connectedness? With this feeling of being wholly connected comes empathy and compassion. As we have said, transformation within the individual precedes any hoped-for impact on the larger community.

"Every person has the capacity to think independent of circumstances," says Beckwith. Each of us on the planet may envision any condition we wish by conscious choice. If we envision the right condition, we get to express the greatest part of our individual potentials. Human beings are more than indigenous to a particular climate or region. As human beings, Ralph Waldo Emerson reminded us, we are endogenous. We can create our own environment. You do not have to wait for anything to change in order for you to be you. As co-creators with the universe we create our own climate, environment, or inner terrain. Thus, you get to create your own ethical tonality for peace, nonviolence, reconciliation, and inner connectedness.

There is no "other." The so-called "other" is ourselves. The words brother and mother contain the word "other." The so-called "other" is potentially your brother or potentially your mother. There is only one mind.[21] This is why Glen Rein, a biochemist, tells us that prayer can change DNA a continent away. Is it not marvelous that when you cooperate with ultimate good, you become one with Infinite Spirit? We are one with nature, people, plants, and animals in their hunger, pain, and pleasure.

Edgar Sheffield Brightman tells us that the highest level of spirituality is cooperation. If we have cooperation in our bodies we call that health; if we have cooperation in society between institutions, corporations, and governments we call that civilization; if we are able to observe cooperation in the cosmos, we experience the four seasons and identify the constellations.[22]

Hubbard tells us that our species has gained the power to destroy all life systems within 32 years, or to use our ethical, social, spiritual, scientific, and technological powers to take us to the cusp of being the cooperation, the peace, and the reconciliation we wish to see.

How can we cause the light of compassion, courage, and wisdom to shine on the challenges and conflicts of the world? Edith Wharton said, "There are two ways of spreading light: to be the candle or the mirror that reflects it." If the world we are seeing is not to our liking, there is only one thing to do: work on ourselves. Nothing is happening *to* you; it is all of your own conscious creation.

THE IMPERATIVE FOR HIGHER EDUCATION

Ikeda says, "What our world most requires now is the kind of education that fosters love for human kind, that develops character, that provides an intellectual basis for the realization of peace and empowers learners to contribute to improve society."

These are his foundational principles for Soka University of Japan and Soka University of America, both first-class institutions, founded by Ikeda on pedagogies of peace.

In light of Ikeda's requirements for the academy, Clark Kerr's *Uses of the University* and the current international orientation to violence, what are the consequences if global society and the university decide to remain unchanged or silent? What are the consequences for coming generations? What are the global ethical issues? What are the roles university presidents ought to play? Who are the effective models of ethical leadership in the history of the American academy? What are the obstacles and opportunities to university presidents becoming strong leaders in promoting global ethics? And how can we renew the University presidency as a focus of moral agency in global society?

If human society continues on its current trajectory, we will see an increasingly rapid exhaustion of natural resources, increasingly serious difficulties related to global climate change, difficulties in providing food for all, a continued degradation of the earth, new variations on disease and premature death, more conflicts and wars, out-of-control human technologies, a breakdown in the atmosphere of social harmony between generations, and more under-achieving colleges where students should be learning more and more. Tragically, we are currently experiencing *Excellence Without A Soul* in the academy, says Harry R. Lewis.[24]

The Oxford Conclave on Global Ethics, held in September 2005, gave birth to a movement to address this last problem. Gathered at the University of Oxford in England, presidents and deans from universities across America agreed that we must develop a consciousness and commitment to improving the ethical foundation of undergraduate education using Derek Bok's core purposes: learning to communicate, learning to think critically, building good character, preparing for citizenship, living with diversity, preparing for a global society, developing a breadth of interests, and preparing for a career. If this movement fails and no other effort comes forth, there will be continuation of the serious breakdown we are witnessing as the universities go from "*ivyleague.edu*" to "*ivyleague.com*," in the words of Howard Gardner.

Adult generations are not only failing in their responsibilities to youth, but are also resisting reform. Adult generations continue to run up huge governmental debts and obligations. They now want to pay off these debts by accelerating the liquidation and consumption of earth's natural resources; they have introduced toxins into the environment that caused serious damage to biological systems of children and other life; and now they do not want to take responsibility for their malfeasance and misfeasance.

Carl J. Casebolt reminds us that large economic institutions are frequently accountable only to their major stockholders and sometimes not even accountable to them. He states:

[A]mong the top 100 entities generating the largest cash flows, half are nations and the other half are corporations. Wal-Mart generates more cash than the gross national product of Greece. What does this mean? When Wal-Mart wants certain legislation passed, what kind of influence will they have? We have allowed, as Ralph Nader shows, large corporate entities to buy enormous influence with politicians. It seems that politicians will respond to the will of corporate entities, provided that they get their funding. Unless and until corporate resources are taken out of elections, I don't see much hope for democracy. What we have now is a plutocracy. People or corporations with money make the laws." A strong case of globally applied ethics would be helpful.[25]

Casebolt also tells us that:

The prevailing public philosophy has gained its supremacy through a mixture of philosophies and ideals that emphasize the creativity of *Homo sapiens,* the seeming limitless supply of natural resources and the seemly infinite capacity of the earth to rejuvenate itself. The advent of mega technologies such as nuclear energy, computer-assistant intelligence, and biotechnology have tended to enhance the view that there need be not limits to progress, no limits to resource use and no limits to the earth ability to absorb hazardous waste.[26]

Casebolt's "globally applied ethics" must be defined and fostered on the campuses of our colleges and universities; otherwise, explosions will occur on our campuses as youths become aware of the facts concerning the state of the planet. There seems to be no embarrassment about the present reality and what it portends for the earth and future generations. Citizen authority must be restored in labor laws, environmental laws, and public safety laws—or the resulting unhappiness, disenchantment, and campus riots will be worse than the 1999 Seattle Washington riot against the World Trade Organization.

University presidents must deeply concern themselves with the global ethical issue of calling for an intergenerational justice compact. The work begun among university leaders at The Oxford Conclave has the best chance for getting a campaign for intergenerational justice launched in the American academy while challenging students and faculties to be the change they wish to see. This is the best and only solution to improve or alleviate problems between generations. Future generations are not abstractions; they need justice by current generations. I believe that only an honest encounter with truth will help us constructively deal with present realities.

Why has child poverty in the United States gone from 15 percent ten years ago to 20 percent now? Should not our youth get a sensitive response to how to reverse this trend? College students must understand what is happening without reacting with anger or violence to the crisis. The virtues of compassion, forgiveness, healing, and reconciliation are needed, and all must be aware that change is called for or there is going to be greater tension between parents and children globally. Good examples include the youth unrest in the nation of France; the London subway bombings by British-born youths; the American immigration issue; the issues of Hurricane Katrina; the uses of the U.S. Constitution; and the thwarted terrorist plot involving 17 Toronto-area youths.

We must have the will to be aware of what has been done that is unjust. Society has accepted too much without questioning. By raising questions in the academy concerning the interconnectedness of social policy and the need for value creation, university presidents can begin the process of an informed reconciliation between the generations. The Oxford Conclave conceived new strategies to effectively deal with communal, individual, institutional, and national denial.

ROLE MODELS FOR 21st-CENTURY UNIVERSITY LEADERSHIP

Let me conclude by pointing to a world-renowned university president and an internationally recognized college president of the 20th century, both of whom distinguished themselves for providing inspired ethical leadership to their respective campuses and as engaged global citizens.[27] Both were aware that the intergenerational crisis required the use of ethics as a science of ideals.

Benjamin Elijah Mays, president of Morehouse College from 1940 to 1967, made ethical, educational, social and theological criticisms permeate his writings, from *The Crisis* and *The Christian Century* to *The Journal of Educational Sociology* and *The Christian Science Monitor*. There exists no modern-day parallel among college presidents from an ethical perspective. It should be noted, however, that Robert Maynard Hutchins, president of The University of Chicago from 1929 to 1951, is believed by many to be the greatest university president of the 20th century.

As Hutchins was The University of Chicago, Mays was Morehouse College. Like Hutchins, Mays' unblinking realism never yielded to cynicism or nihilism. Both men were constant optimists. But, unlike Hutchins, Mays was not just heard—he was honored as an unarmed prophet who disarmed Jim Crow and created African-American leaders in a laboratory of freedom at Morehouse College. Lerone Bennett says, "Mays did with pennies, nickels and dimes, what Harvard, Yale and Chicago did with millions." Indeed, there are enough parallels between Hutchins and Mays to suspect a significant, shared influence:

1. Hutchins was a good debater. He learned his method at Oberlin and relied on it throughout his life. Mays was a champion debater at Bates, where he was also captain of the team in his senior year. He later taught debating at Morehouse for three years to teams that were never defeated.
2. Hutchins eliminated intercollegiate football at Chicago; Mays wanted to end it at Morehouse.
3. Hutchins spoke publicly about educational problems, politics, freedom, and democracy, delivering nearly eight hundred public addresses from the 1930s to the 1950s. His dynamism and oratory shaped the public image of The University of Chicago; Mays addressed the issues of segregation, politics, religion, education, and democracy, delivering over 800 public addresses from the 1940s to the 1970s. The power of his eloquence stamped the Morehouse mystique as a builder of leaders.
4. Hutchins authored twelve books on democracy, education, freedom, and the world state; Mays authored nine books on the church, God, race relations, and the social gospel.
5. In 1937, Hutchins convinced the faculty and trustees to admit high school juniors; in 1942, Mays established an early recruitment program, which lured Martin Luther King Jr. and Maynard Holbrook Jackson Jr. to Morehouse College after their junior years in high school.

6. Hutchins created an atmosphere in which everyone around him was moved to do his best work, because it was expected of him. Mays was known for saying,

> There is an air of expectancy at Morehouse College. It is expected that the student who enters here will do well. It is also expected that once a man bears the insignia of a Morehouse graduate, he will do exceptionally well.

7. Hutchins defined the ends he sought according to an ethical ideal as did Mays.
8. Hutchins was described as a "man of honor," who "tried to live up to his convictions." Mays was called "walking integrity."
9. Kerr called Hutchins "the last of the giants" to rule American universities; Lerone Bennett called Mays "the last of the great school masters."
10. The faculty at The University of Chicago did not want Hutchins to leave in 1951; the faculty of Morehouse College refused to accept May's decision to retire in 1965 and asked him to stay on for two more years, until the centennial of the College.
11. Hutchins quoted heavily from the great books of the western world; Mays quoted from the classical literature of African Americans and from the Harvard Classics.
12. "I have assumed," Hutchins wrote in 1956, "that the duty of an educator is to try to change things from the way they are to the way they ought to be." On becoming president of Morehouse, in 1940, Mays announced, "I intend to draw more than my breath and my salary." Hutchins led the "great Chicago fight." Mays led the "unending Morehouse debate."

It was in the spirit and tradition of Mays and Hutchins that leaders of universities from across America engaged in five days of deep dialogue in September 2005 at England's University of Oxford, the cradle of western higher education. They took seriously the responsibilities of the university to address the daunting ethical issues facing the global 21st century. And together they articulated a courageous declaration, agreeing to reconvene a year later to hold each other accountable for enacting these principles at their respective institutions. Here, in their eloquent words, are principles to which they call all university leaders to commit:

Declaration of The Oxford Conclave on Global Ethics

The beliefs that follow are rooted in the irrefutable fact of the interdependence of all people, which requires exercise of ethical behavior for the common good. In recognition of the fact that we live in an increasingly complex world, there is a strong imperative for global ethical leadership.

Ethics is a timeless concept, yet more relevant than ever. It has universal, rather than narrow or partisan, connotations. It is essentially a belief that just behavior, honorable behavior, unselfish behavior—in other words, character in action—must permeate all sectors of society. Translating this belief into action will ensure a more promising future.

Since higher education will prepare most of the people who will help shape the future of the world, it must partner with other societal institutions such as the family, community, spiritual support systems, primary and secondary schools, business, local, state, and federal governments, non-profit organizations, and philanthropic entities, to provide a leadership role in this worthy endeavor.

Statement of Beliefs and Responsibilities

We believe that higher education has the responsibility to:

1. Increase access to quality education for all citizens of the world
2. Emphasize and support research that provides solutions to present and future challenges affecting the global society
3. Broaden and deepen the traditional service mission of universities to engage the human and environmental issues of the twenty-first century
4. Further the time-honored mission of universities in a continuous and more vigorous search for truth and meaning
5. Actively model and demonstrate civil discourse and ethical leadership
6. Protect and advance universally accepted standards of ethical behavior;
7. Introduce all students to interdisciplinary approaches to learning that stress connectedness and emphasize potential solutions to global issues
8. Foster, among our colleagues and students, the capacity for moral reasoning and awareness of long-term consequences of choices, i.e., moral imagination
9. Develop, among our students, the future leaders of society:
    i.   Desire—and the interdisciplinary methods and tools—for meaningful, informed engagement with the critical social issues of our time
    ii.   Skills for nonviolent, productive conflict resolution
    iii. Commitment to ethical leadership
    iv.   Ethical basis and strategies for discovering individual meaning and purpose, expediting progress toward a just global society.
    —Adopted in September 2005 at the University of Oxford, England

Notes

FOREWORD AND INTRODUCTION

1. Jimmy Carter, *Sources of Strength* (New York: Random House/Times Books, 1997), 191.

2. See Erik R. Peterson, "Scanning More Distant Horizons," Chapter 1, this book.

3. Ray Kurzweil, "The Law of Accelerating Returns," *KurzweilAI.net*, March 7, 2001, http://www.kurzweilai.net/articles/art0134.html?printable=1 (accessed October 27, 2006).

4. Jonathan Glover, *Humanity: A Moral History of the Twentieth Century* (New Haven, CT: Yale University Press, 2002), 6.

5. David Hollenbach, "Christian Ethics and The Common Good," *Woodstock Report*, June 2003, No. 74, http://woodstock.georgetown.edu/publications/report/r-fea74.htm (accessed October 27, 2006).

6. Frances Hesselbein, *Hesselbein on Leadership* (San Francisco, CA: Jossey-Bass, 2002), 131–2.

CHAPTER 1

1. See, for example, the process by which the Copenhagen Consensus conclusions were reached. Both the processes and the recommendations of the deliberations of a number of Nobel Laureates and others associated with the effort are set out in Bjørn Lomborg, *Global Crises, Global Solutions* (Cambridge and New York: Cambridge University Press, 2004). See also http://www.copenhagenconsensus.com.

2. For a progress report on the UN Millennium Challenge Goals, see UN Statistics Division, "Progress towards the Millennium Development Goals, 1990–2005," June 13, 2005, http://unstats.un.org/unsd/mi/mi_coverfinal.htm (accessed October 27, 2006). See also "Millennium Development Goals, Targets and Indicators," in World Bank Group, World Development Indicators 2005, http://devdata.worldbank.org/wdi2005/Cover.htm (accessed October 27, 2006).

3. See United Nations, Department of Economic and Social Affairs, Population Division, *World Urbanization Prospects: The 2003 Revision*, March 2004, http://www.un.org/esa/population/publications/wup2003/WUP2003.htm (accessed October 27, 2006).

4. Defined as living two hundred kilometers or less from a coastline. See n 4.

5. United Nations, Department of Economic and Social Affairs, Population Division, *International Migration Report 2002*, http://www.un.org/esa/population/publications/ittmig2002/ittmigrep2002.htm (accessed October 27, 2006).

6. Ibid.

7. United Nations, *The Millennium Development Goals Report 2005*, http://www.un.org/Docs/summit2005/MDGBook.pdf (accessed October 27, 2006).

8. Ibid., 8.

9. Ania Lichtarowicz, " 'Millions more starving' by 2015," *BBC News*, February 17, 2006, http://news.bbc.co.uk/1/hi/world/4724282.stm (accessed October 27, 2006). The article reported on projections made during a panel of the American Association for the Advancement of Science annual meeting in St. Louis.

10. United Nations Environment Programme, "Vital Water Graphics," http://www.unep.org/vitalwater/ (accessed October 27, 2006).

11. Sandra L. Postel, "Water for Food Production: Will There Be Enough in 2025?" *BioScience* 48, no. 8 (1998): 629–37.

12. Organisation for Economic Co-operation and Development, International Energy Agency, *World Energy Outlook 2004* (OECD: Paris, 2004), http://www.iea.org/textbase/nppdf/free/2004/weo2004.pdf (accessed October 27, 2006).

13. Organisation for Economic Co-operation and Development, International Energy Agency, *World Energy Outlook 2005-Middle East and North Africa Insights* (OECD: Paris, 2004).

14. *The National Interest*, no. 82 (Winter 2005): 21.

15. Thomas Ricker, "IBM's Blue Gene/L: world's fastest supercomputer at 280.6 teraflops," *Engadget*, October 28, 2005, http://www.engadget.com/2005/10/28/ibms-blue-gene-l-worlds-fastest-supercomputer-at-280-6/ (accessed October 27, 2006). See also TOP500 Supercomputer Sites, http://www.top500.org/.

16. See https://www3.nationalgeographic.com/genographic/index.html.

17. Thomas L. Friedman, *The World is Flat: A Brief History of the Twenty-First Century* (New York: Farrar, Straus and Giroux, 2005).

18. "Coming of Age," *The Economist*, January 21–27, 2006.

19. "Dreaming with BRICS: The Path to 2050," *Goldman Sachs*, October 2003, http://www.gs.com/insight/research/reports/99.pdf (accessed October 27, 2006).

20. Cited in John Naisbitt, *Global Paradox* (New York: William Morrow and Company, 1994), 19.

21. "Mapping the Global Future," *National Intelligence Council*, December 2004, 29, http://www.dni.gov/nic/NIC_globaltrend2020.html (accessed October 27, 2006).

22. See, for example, Erik R. Peterson, "Surrender to Markets," *The Washington Quarterly* 18, no. 4 (Autumn 1995) and Erik R. Peterson, "Looming Collision of Capitalisms?" *The Washington Quarterly* 17, no. 1 (Spring 1994).

23. Joseph A. Schumpeter, *Capitalism, Socialism and Democracy* (New York: Harper, 1975) 82–85.

24. 2004 Transparency International Survey of fifty thousand in sixty-four countries by Gallup International, http://ww1.transparency.org/surveys/barometer/dnld/barometer_report_8_12_2004.pdf (accessed October 27, 2006).

25. http://www.theglobalfund.org/en/.

CHAPTER 2

1. Howard Gardner, Mihaly Csikszentmihalyi, and William Damon, *Good Work: When Excellence and Ethics Meet* (New York: Basic Books, 2001).

2. John Gardner, interview by William Damon, December 15, 1999.

3. John Gardner, interview by William Damon, July 10, 2000.

4. See n 2.

5. See n 3.

6. Rushworth M. Kidder, *Shared Values for a Troubled World: Conversations with Men and Women of Conscience* (San Francisco, CA: Jossey-Bass Publishers, 1994), 135.

7. Ibid., 136.

8. Ibid., 137.

9. William Drayton, interview by William Damon, January 16, 2001.

10. Ibid.

11. Yo-Yo Ma. Silk Road Project. 2005. Vision Statement. http://www.silkroad-project.org/about/vision.html (accessed September 13, 2005).

12. Elizabeth Ten Grotenhuis, ed., *Along the Silk Road* (Washington, DC: University of Washington Press, 2003), 35.

13. Ibid., 36–37.

14. See n 6.

15. Derek Bok, *Universities in the Marketplace: The Commercialization of Higher Education* (Princeton, NJ: Princeton University Press, 2003), 15.

16. See n 9.

17. Wendy Fischman et al., *Making Good: How Young People Cope with Moral Dilemmas at Work* (Cambridge, MA: Harvard University Press, 2004).

18. Confidential interview by Carrie James and Tanya Rose, May 5, 2004.

19. See n 15.

20. See n 6.

21. Ibid., 199.

22. Ibid.

23. The Good Work Project. GoodWork® Toolkit. http://www.goodworkproject.org/toolkit.htm (accessed September 13, 2005).

24. See n 3.

25. Anita Roddick, interview by Mollie Galloway and *Francie Green*, April 22, 1999.

CHAPTER 3

1. Deval L. Patrick, "Crisis as a Platform for Change: Lessons from Coke and Corporate America" (paper presented at "Leading With Integrity" program series, The Southern Institute for Business and Professional Ethics, October 22, 2004).

2. World Economic Forum, "Trust in Governments, Corporations and Global Institutions Continues to Decline," *World Economic Forum*, December 15, 2005, http://www.weforum.org/en/media/Latest%20Press%20Releases/PRESSRE-LEASES87 (accessed October 28, 2006).

3. World Economic Forum, "Global Survey on Trust, 2002" (www.weforum.org). Findings were based on a poll involving fifteen thousand in-person or telephone interviews across mainly "Group of 20" countries: Argentina, Australia, Brazil, Canada, Chile, China, France, Germany, United Kingdom, India, Indonesia, Italy, Mexico, Nigeria, Russia, South Africa, Spain, Turkey, Uruguay, and United States. See also "States 'not run by people's will,'" *BBC News*, September 14, 2005, http://news.bbc.co.uk/2/hi/europe/4247158.stm (accessed October 28, 2006). The survey of fifty thousand people worldwide found that only 23 percent trust politicians, while religious leaders rank as the most trusted group.

4. Zogby International, "U.S. Public Widely Distrusts Its Leaders—Lichtman/Zogby Interactive poll: Gov't., Corporate Scandals Damage Public Trust in Institutions at the Bedrock of Society," *Zogby International*, May 23, 2006, http://www.zogby.com/news/ReadNews.dbm?ID=1116 (accessed October 28, 2006). See also DecisionQuest, "Reuters/DecisionQuest Poll Shows Most Americans Have Lost Trust in Leaders Over the Last Four Years," *DecisionQuest*, September 29, 2004, http://www.decisionquest.com/press_center.php?NewsID=97 (accessed October 28, 2006).

5. See The Harris Poll® #4, January 13, 2005, "Fewer Americans Than Europeans Have Trust in the Media—Press, Radio and TV," *HarrisInteractive*, http://www.harrisinteractive.com/harris_poll/index.asp?PID=534 (accessed October 28, 2006) and Paul C. Light, "Trust in Charitable Organizations," Reform Watch Brief No. 6, *The Brookings Institution*, December 2002, http://www.brookings.edu/comm/reformwatch/rw06.htm (accessed October 28, 2006).

6. Melvin L. DeFleur and Sandra Ball-Rokeach, *Theories of Mass Communication* (New York: Longman, 1989), 258–69.

7. "Worldwide Internet Users Top 1 Billion in 2005," *Computer Industry Almanac*, January 4, 2006, http://www.c-i-a.com/pr0106.htm (accessed October 28, 2006).

8. Paula Marshall, "Trust across the Power Divide: A Study of the Edna McConnell Clark Foundation," GoodWork Project Report Series 42, Harvard University, 2005, p. 1, http://pzweb.harvard.edu/eBookstore/PDFs/GoodWork42.pdf (accessed October 28, 2006).

9. Robert D. Putnam, *Making Democracy Work: Civic Traditions in Modern Italy* (Princeton, NJ: Princeton University Press, 1993), 261–85.

10. Richard W Smith, "Servant Leadership: A Pathway to the Emerging Territory," in *Reflections on Leadership: How Robert K. Greenleaf's Theory of Servant-Leadership Influenced Today's Top Management Thinkers*, ed. Larry C. Spears (New York: Wiley, 1995), 199–216.

11. James S. Coleman, *Foundations of Social Theory* (Cambridge, MA: Harvard University Press, 1990), 311.

12. Robert Levering, *A Great Place to Work: What Makes Some Employers so Good (and Most so Bad)* (San Francisco, CA: Great Place to Work Institute, 2000), 264–5.

13. See Tony Simons, "The High Cost of Lost Trust," *Harvard Business Review*, September 2002.

14. Kurt T. Dirks and Daniel Skarlicki, "Trust in Leaders: Existing Research and Emerging Issues," in *Trust and Distrust in Organizations: Dilemmas and Approaches*, ed. Roderick M. Kramer and Karen S. Cook (New York: Russell Sage Foundation, 2004).

15. Joshua Joseph, *National Business Ethics Survey: How Employees View Ethics in Their Organizations* (Washington, DC: Ethics Resource Center, 2003).

16. See Afsaneh Nahavandi, *The Art and Science of Leadership* (Upper Saddle River, NJ: Prentice Hall, 2000).

17. See Carl Rhodes and Rick Wilson, "Leaders, Followers, and the Institutional Problem of Trust" (paper presented at the Trust Working Group Meeting, Russell Sage Foundation, New York, NY, February 19–20, 1999).

18. Joseph L. Badaracco Jr., *Leading Quietly* (Boston, MA: Harvard Business School Press, 2002), 27.

19. Max De Pree, *Leading Without Power: Finding Hope in Serving Community* (Holland, MI: Shepherd Foundation, 1997), 121–35.

20. James B. Tatum, "Meditations on Servant Leadership," in *Reflections on Leadership: How Robert K. Greenleaf's Theory of Servant-Leadership Influenced Today's Top Management Thinkers*, ed. Larry C. Spears (New York: Wiley, 1995), 308–12.

21. Quoted in G. Jeffrey MacDonald, "Critics.Com," *The Atlanta Journal-Constitution*, May 27 2006, sec. B, p. 1.

22. Ryan Mahoney, "Coke Gets Slammed on Wikipedia," *Atlanta Business Chronicle*, June 9, 2006, sec. A, p. 1, http://www.bizjournals.com/atlanta/stories/2006/06/12/story3.html (accessed October 28, 2006).

23. Daniel Goleman et al., *Primal Leadership: Realizing the Power of Emotional Intelligence* (Boston: Harvard Business School Press, 2002), 30–31.

24. CEOs as a group score lower than all others in the workforce in emotional intelligence, according to research involving more than five hundred thousand people. See Travis Bradberry and Jean Greaves, "Heartless Bosses?" *Harvard Business Review*, December 2005.

25. Frances Hesselbein and Eric K. Shinseki, *Be-Know-Do: Leadership The Army Way* (San Francisco: Jossey-Bass, 2004), xv.

CHAPTER 4

1. Peter F. Drucker, *The Effective Executive* (Burlington, MA: Butterworth-Heinemann, 1999).

2. Peter F. Drucker, "What Business Can Learn from Nonprofits," *Harvard Business Review* 67, no. 4 (1989): 88.

CHAPTER 7

1. Paul Hawken, *The Ecology of Commerce: A Declaration of Sustainability* (New York: HarperBusiness, 1993).

2. Ibid., 25.

3. Ray C. Anderson, *Mid-Course Correction: Toward a Sustainable Enterprise* (Atlanta: Peregrinzilla Press/Chelsea Green Publishers, 1998).

4. Aldo Leopold, *Game Management* (New York: Charles Scribner's Sons, 1933).

5. Rachel Carson, *Silent Spring* (Boston, MA: Houghton Mifflin, 1962).

6. See http://www.interfacesustainability.com.

7. Janine M. Benyus, *Biomimicry: Innovation Inspired by Nature* (New York: William Morrow and Co., 1997).

8. Abraham H. Maslow, *Motivation and Personality*. 3rd ed. (New York: Harper and Row, 1987).

9. Glenn Thomas, ©1996.

CHAPTER 8

1. Thomas Malthus, *Essay on the Principle of Population* (London: St. Paul's Church Yard, 1798).

2. K. J. Boote et al., *Physiology and Determination of Crop Yield* (Madison, WI: American Society of Agronomy, 1994).

3. Ibid.

4. *The State of Food Insecurity in the World-2005* (Rome: Food and Agriculture Organization of the United Nations, 2005).

5. *5th Report on the World Nutrition Situation: Nutrition for Improved Development Outcomes* (Geneva: United Nations Standing Committee on Nutrition, 2004).

6. Joachim von Braun, *The World Food Situation* (Washington, DC: International Food Policy Research Institute, 2005).

7. See n 2.

8. Ibid.

9. World Commission on Environment and Development, *Our Common Future* (New York: Oxford Press, 1987).

10. World Commission on Environmental Development, *Food: 2000. Global Policies for Sustainable Agriculture* (London: Zed Books, 1987).

11. See n 2.

12. Ibid.

13. E. T. York et al., "An Assessment of Strategic Opportunities for Sustainable Agricultural Intensifications in Sub-Saharan Africa" (unpublished report, available from U.S. A.I.D., Washington, D.C., and Carter Center, Atlanta, Georgia, 1997).

14. G8 Gleneagles 2005, Perthshire, Scotland, July 6–8, 2005.

15. E. T. York et al., "Strategies for Accelerating Agricultural Development. A Report of the Presidential Mission on Agricultural Development in Egypt" (unpublished report, available from U.S. A.I.D., Washington, D.C., and Ministry of Agriculture, Cairo, Egypt, 1982).

16. E. T. York et al., "The National Agricultural Resource Project—An Assessment for a Cooperative Agreement Between the Government of Egypt and the Government of the U.S.A." (unpublished report, available from U.S. A.I.D., Washington, D.C., and Ministry of Agriculture, Cairo, Egypt, 1994).

17. E. T. York et al., "Agricultural Development and Economic Progress in the Caribbean Basin. Report of the Presidential Mission on Agricultural Development in the Caribbean" (unpublished report, available from U.S. A.I.D., Washington, D.C., 1980).

18. Claire Andre and Manuel Velasquez, "World Hunger: A Moral Response," *Issues in Ethics* 5, no. 1 (Spring 1992), http://www.scu.edu/ethics/publications/iie/v5n1/hunger.html (accessed October 28, 2006).

19. Clark Ford, "Syllabus: Ethics and World Hunger," Iowa State University, http://www.public.iastate.edu/%7Ejwcwolf/ClassSyllabi/hon321u.html (accessed October 28, 2006).

20. See n 18.

21. Peter Singer, "Famine, Affluence, and Morality," *Philosophy and Public Affairs* 1, no. 3 (1972): 229–43.

22. Ibid.

23. Joachim von Braun, "Ethics and the Global Food System," International Food Policy Research Institute Forum, 2004, http://www.ifpri.org/pubs/newsletters/ifpriforum/200412/if09commentary.htm (accessed October 28, 2006).

24. Baylor University, "Food and Hunger," The Center For Christian Ethics, http://www.baylor.edu/christianethics/index.php?id=23038 (accessed October 28, 2006).

CHAPTER 9

1. American Council on Education, "Facts In Brief: Postsecondary Enrollment Expected to Increase As College-Aged Population Rises," http://www.acenet.edu/AM/Template.cfm?Section=Search&template=/CM/HTMLDisplay.cfm&ContentID=4113 (accessed October 28, 2006).

2. See Erik R. Peterson, "Scanning More Distant Horizons," Chapter 1, this book.

3. Thomas L. Friedman, *The World is Flat: A Brief History of the Twenty-First Century* (New York: Farrar, Straus and Giroux, 2005), 48–72.

4. Ibid.

5. Erik R. Peterson, *Seven Revolutions: Looking Out to the Year 2025* (Washington, DC: Global Strategy Institute at the Center for Strategic and International Studies, 2006), http://www.7revs.org.

6. Ibid.

7. Friedman, *The World is Flat*, 173–200.

8. Ibid., 256–75.

9. Ibid., 327–249.

10. Ibid., 382–884.

11. Lee Bollinger, "Remarks for 2005 Commencement Exercises," Columbia University, May 18, 2005, http://www.columbia.edu/cu/news/05/05/president_speech.html (accessed October 28, 2006).

12. American Association of University Professors' Statement on Academic Freedom, http://www.aaup.org/AAUP/statements/Redbook/1940stat.htm.

13. The Association of American Colleges and Universities' statement on Academic Freedom and Educational Responsibility, accessed online at http://www.aacu-edu.org/about/statements/academic_freedom.cfm.

14. Beheruz N. Sethna, "The Search for Peace and Humility," *The International Journal of Humanities and Peace* 20, no. 1 (2004): 8.

CHAPTER 10

1. H. Etzkowitz and L. Leyesdorff, "Introduction: Universities in the Global Knowledge Economy," in *Universities and the Global Knowledge Economy: A Triple Helix of University-Industry-Government Relations*, ed. H. Etzkowitz and L. Leyesdorff (London: Pinter, 1997), 1–8.

2. Thomas L. Friedman, *The World is Flat: A Brief History of the Twenty-First Century* (New York: Farrar, Straus and Giroux, 2005).

3. Albert-Laszlo Barabasi, *Linked: The New Science of Networks* (Cambridge, MA: Perseus Publishing, 2002).

4. Mark C. Taylor, *The Moment of Complexity: Emerging Network Culture* (Chicago, IL: University of Chicago Press, 2001).

5. Corynne McSherry, *Who Owns Academic Work? Battling for Control of Intellectual Property* (Cambridge, MA: Harvard University Press, 2001).

6. David L. Kirp, *Shakespeare, Einstein, and The Bottom Line: The Marketing of Higher Education* (Cambridge, MA: Harvard University Press, 2003); Sheila Slaughter and Larry L. Leslie, *Academic Capitalism: Politics, Policies, and The Entrepreneurial University* (Baltimore, MD: Johns Hopkins University Press, 1997).

7. Jared L. Bleak, *When For-Profit Meets Nonprofit: Educating through the Market* (New York: Routledge, 2005).

8. Stuart L. Hart, *Capitalism at the Crossroads: The Unlimited Business Opportunities in Solving the World's Most Difficult Problems* (Upper Saddle River, NJ: Wharton School Publishing, 2005); C. K. Prahalad, *The Fortune at the Bottom of the Pyramid: Eradicating Poverty through Profits* (Upper Saddle River, NJ: Wharton School Publishing, 2004).

9. Prahalad, *The Fortune at the Bottom of the Pyramid.*

10. L. D. Brown, "Creating Social Capital: Nongovernmental Development Organizations and Intersectoral Problem Solving," in *Private Action and the Public Good*, ed. W. W. Powell and E. S. Clemens (New Haven, CT: Yale University Press, 1998), 228–41.

11. M. Mumper, "The Paradox of College Prices: Five Stories with No Clear Lesson," in *The States and Public Higher Education Policy: Affordability, Access, and Accountability*, ed. D. E. Heller (Baltimore, MD: Johns Hopkins University Press, 2001), 39–63.

12. Kirp, *Shakespeare, Einstein, and The Bottom Line.*

13. E. M. M. Valentin, "University–Industry Cooperation: A Framework of Benefits and Obstacles," *Industry and Higher Education*, 14, no. 3 (2000): 165–72.

14. M. Gulbrandsen, "Universities and Industrial Competitive Advantage," in *Universities and the Global Knowledge Economy: A Triple Helix of University-Industry-Government Relations*, ed. H. Etzkowitz and L. Leyesdorff (London: Pinter, 1997), 121–31; T. Turpin and S. Garrett-Jones, "Innovation Networks in Australia and China," in *Universities and the Global Knowledge Economy: A Triple Helix of University-Industry-Government Relations*, ed. H. Etzkowitz and L. Leyesdorff (London: Pinter, 1997), 21–32.

15. R. M. Kanter, "Collaborative Advantage: The Art of Alliances," *Harvard Business Review*, 72, no. 4 (1994): 96–108.

16. Yves L. Doz and Gary Hamel, *Alliance Advantage: The Art of Creating Value through Partnering* (Boston, MA: Harvard Business School Press, 1998).

17. See n 10.

18. C. P. Snow, *The Two Cultures and the Scientific Revolution* (Cambridge, MA: Cambridge University Press, 1959).

19. J. J. Duderstadt, "Delicate Balance: Market Forces versus the Public Interest," in *Buying In or Selling Out: The Commercialization of the American Research University*, ed. D. G. Stein (New Brunswick, NJ: Rutgers University Press, 2004), 56–74, 72.

20. Z. W. Hall, "The Academy and Industry: A View Across the Divide," in *Buying In or Selling Out: The Commercialization of the American Research University*, ed. D. G. Stein (New Brunswick, NJ: Rutgers University Press, 2004), 153–160.

21. Jennifer Washburn, *University, Inc.: The Corporate Corruption of American Higher Education* (New York: Basic Books, 2005).

22. James Engell and Anthony Dangerfield, *Saving Higher Education in the Age of Money* (Charlottesville, VA: University of Virginia Press, 2005).

23. Kwame Anthony Appiah, *Cosmopolitanism: Ethics in a World of Strangers* (New York: W. W. Norton and Company, 2006).

24. Talcott Parsons, *Structure and Process in Modern Societies* (Glencoe, IL: Free Press, 1960).

25. See n 16.

26. Robert Phillips, *Stakeholder Theory and Organizational Ethics* (San Francisco, CA: Berrett-Koehler Publishers, 2003).

27. Goldie Blumenstyk, "Yale Decides to End Investments in Oil Companies Operating in Sudan Because of Abuses in Darfur Region," *Chronicle of Higher Education*, http://chronicle.com/daily/2006/02/2006021706n.htm (accessed February 27, 2006); Erin Strout, "Stanford U. divests stocks in 4 companies that do business in Sudan," *Chronicle of Higher Education*, http://chronicle.com/daily/2005/06/2005061303n.htm (accessed February 27, 2006).

28. James O. Freedman, *Liberal Education & The Public Interest* (Iowa City, IA: University of Iowa Press, 2003), 33.

29. James R. Davis, *Learning to Lead: A Handbook for Postsecondary Administrators* (Westport, CT: ACE/Praeger, 2003), 116.

30. Ibid.

31. Joan Poliner Shapiro and Jacqueline A. Stefkovich, *Ethical Leadership and Decision Making in Education: Applying Theoretical Perspectives to Complex Dilemmas*. 2nd ed. (Mahwah, NJ: Lawrence Erlbaum Associates, 2005).

32. See, for example, Craig E. Johnson, *Meeting the Ethical Challenges of Leadership* (Thousand Oaks, CA: Sage, 2001); W. May, ed., *Ethics and Higher Education* (New York: ACE/Macmillan, 1990); George B. Vaughan, *Dilemmas of Leadership: Decision Making and Ethics in the Community College* (San Francisco, CA: Jossey-Bass, 1992).

33. David D. Chrislip and Carl E. Larson, *Collaborative Leadership: How Citizens and Civic Leaders can Make a Difference* (San Francisco, CA: Jossey-Bass, 1994).

CHAPTER 11

1. The "old spirituality" is described by Bishop John Shelby Spong, who focuses on the virtues of integrity, compassion, equality, and faith in his 22nd published book titled *The Sins of Scripture: Exposing the Bible's Texts of Hate to Reveal the God of Love*. Yet he also reveals how the Bible was used to oppose the Magna Carta; support the divine right of kings; to condemn the insights of Galileo and Charles Darwin; to support slavery, apartheid, and segregation; to justify the crusades and their unspeakable horrors against the Muslim people; to justify the murderous behavior of the inquisition; to justify the anti-Semitism of the holocaust; to justify the treating of women as

second-class citizens; to encourage the abuse of children; to support environmental degradation; and to deny justice to gays and lesbian people. See John Shelby Spong, *The Sins of Scripture: Exposing The Bible's Texts of Hate to Reveal the God of Love* (San Francisco: Harper, 2005).

2. Derek Bok, *Our Underachieving Colleges: A Candid Look At How Much Students Learn and Why They Should Be Learning More* (Princeton, NJ: Princeton University Press, 2006), 329.

3. Lawrence Edward Carter Sr., George David Miller, and Neelakanta Radhakrishnan, *Global Ethical Options in the Tradition of Gandhi, King and Ikeda* (New York: Weatherhill, 2001; New Delhi: Gandhi Media Centre, 2004).

4. Matthew Fox, *One River, Many Wells: Wisdom Springing From Global Faiths* (New York: Jeremy P. Tarcher/Putnam, 2000).

5. James W. Fowler, *Stages of Faith: The Psychology of Human Development and the Quest for Meaning* (New York: Harper & Row, 1981), 199–213.

6. Marshall B. Rosenberg, *Nonviolent Communication: A Language of Life* (Encinitas, CO: Puddle Dancer Press, 2003).

7. Andrew Cohen, ed., Carter Phipps—Interview with Duane Elgin, "The Breaking Point," *What is Enlightenment?*, Spring/Summer Issue 19 (2001), 130.

8. Barbara Marx Hubbard, *Conscious Evolution: Awakening the Power of Our Social Potential* (Novato, CA: New World Library, 1998).

9. Our diet is responsible for the United States being the fattest nation on earth. A clogged-up, out-of-balance biosystem produces heart disease, diabetes types 1 and 2, diabetic complications, high blood pressure, arthritis, gallstones, kidney failure, stroke, certain kinds of cancer, acid reflux, other deadly conditions, and spiritual disconnectedness. See Robert O. Young, *The Ph Miracle For Weight Loss: Balance Your Body Chemistry, Achieve Your Ideal Weight* (New York: Warner Books, 2005) 1–25.

10. Ibid., 40.

11. Ibid., 212.

12. Mahatma Gandhi, *Indian Opinion* (South Africa: September 8, 1913).

13. Uma Majmudar, *Gandhi's Pilgrimage of Faith From Darkness to Light* (Albany, NY: Albany State University of New York Press, 2005), 135–7; Eric Itzkin, *Gandhi's Johannesburg Birthplace of Satyagraha* (Johannesburg: Witwalerstand University Press, 2000), 2.

14. James M. Washington, ed., *A Testament of Hope: The Essential Writings and Speeches of Martin Luther King, Jr.* (San Francisco, CA: Harper, 1986), 290.

15. Daisaku Ikeda, *For The Sake of Peace: Seven Paths to Global Harmony* (Santa Monica, CA: Middleway Press, 2002). Daisaku Ikeda, *Soka Education: A Buddhist Vision For Teachers, Students and Parents* (Santa Monica, CA: Middleway Press 2001). Daisaku Ikeda, *Life An Enigma, A Precious Jewel* (New York: Kodansha International, 1982).

16. William W. Purkey and Betty L. Seigel, *Becoming an Invitational Leader: A New Approach to Professional and Personal Success* (Atlanta, GA: Humanics Trade Group, 2003), 1.

17. Frederick J. Streng, Charles L. Lloyd Jr., and Jay T. Allen, *Ways of Being Religious: Readings for a New Approach to Religion* (Englewood Cliffs, NJ: Prentice Hall, 1973), 1.

18. Will Durant and Ariel Durant, *The Story of Civilization: The Age of Napoleon* (New York: MJF Books, 1975), 88–302.

19. Diana L. Eck, *A New Religious America: How a "Christian Country" Has Now Become the World's Most Religiously Diverse Nation* (San Francisco, CA: Harper, 2001), 1–25.

20. Andrew Cohen, "We the Unbelievers..." *What Is Enlightenment?*, June 29, 2005, 144.

21. Ernest Holmes, *The Science of Mind* (New York: Tarcher/Putnam, 1997), 28–29.

22. Edgar Sheffield Brightman, *Nature and Values* (New York: Abingdon-Coresburg Press, 1945), 165.

23. Daisaku Ikeda, "Speech at Rajiv Gandhi Institute for Contemporary Studies," *Living Buddhism* 2, no. 1 (January 1998): 8.

24. Harry R. Lewis, *Excellence Without a Soul: How a Great University Forgot Education* (New York: Public Affairs, 2006).

25. Carl J. Casebolt, with Jackson Lone, *Human Commitment to Earth and Environs: Life and Coming Generations* (Bend, OR: Fourfold Project, 2001), 8.

26. Ibid., 42.

27. Lawrence Edward Carter Sr., ed., *Walking Integrity, Benjamin Elijah Mays, Mentor to Martin Luther King Jr.* (Macon, GA: Mercer University Press, 1998), 11–18.

Index

About the Editor and Contributors

THE EDITOR

John C. Knapp is Professor and Director of The Southern Institute for Business and Professional Ethics at Georgia State University's J. Mack Robinson College of Business. He also serves as a visiting lecturer at the University of Wales, Lampeter, and as an adjunct professor of ethics at Columbia Theological Seminary. Previously, he was Senior Scholar and Professor of Ethical Leadership at Kennesaw State University. Known internationally as an expert in organizational ethics and leadership, he is a frequent speaker and seminar leader, as well as a regular contributor to professional journals, business publications, and broadcast programs.

THE CONTRIBUTORS

Ray C. Anderson is founder and Chairman of Interface Inc., a leading producer and marketer of commercial carpet and fabrics with manufacturing locations on four continents and offices in more than 100 countries. A leading proponent of environmental sustainability, he served as co-chairman of the President's Council on Sustainable Development during the Clinton administration; was recognized by Mikhail Gorbachev with a Millennium Award from Global Green in 1996; and received the George and Cynthia Mitchell International Prize for Sustainable Development in 2001. He is the author of the book, *Mid-Course Correction: Toward a Sustainable Enterprise.*

Lynn Barendsen is a Project Manager on the GoodWork Project at the Harvard Graduate School of Education, an initiative dedicated to the belief that "good work" is at once excellent in technical quality and at the same time responsive to the needs and wishes of the broader community in which it takes place. Since 1997 her research interests have focused in particular on the work of young professionals. She also has taught courses at Boston University in literature and film, English and American literature, and expository writing.

Lawrence Edward Carter Sr. is the first Dean of the Martin Luther King Jr. International Chapel, Professor of Religion, and College Curator at Morehouse College since 1979. He is also the Founder of the Ghandi Institute for Reconciliation. Dr. Carter teaches courses at Morehouse College including Psychology of Religion, Religion and Ethics, and The Life and Thought of Mohandas K. Gandhi and Martin Luther King Jr. He is author of more than 60 publications including the book *Global Ethical Options in the Tradition of Mahatma Gandhi, Martin Luther King, Jr., and Daisaku Ikeda.*

Arun Gandhi is founder and president of The M. K. Gandhi Institute for Nonviolence. The grandson of India's legendary leader, Mohandas K. "Mahatma" Gandhi, he leads programs worldwide aimed at improving the social and economic situations of oppressed people. He is a former journalist with *The Times of India* and is author of five books, most recently *A Testament to Truth*, a collection of his grandfather's writings set in a contemporary context.

Howard Gardner is the John H. and Elisabeth A. Hobbs Professor of Cognition and Education at the Harvard Graduate School of Education. He also holds positions as Adjunct Professor of Psychology at Harvard University and Senior Director of Harvard Project Zero. He received a MacArthur Prize Fellowship in 1981 and is author of over 20 books translated into 24 languages, and several hundred articles. He is best known in educational circles for his theory of multiple intelligences.

Frances Hesselbein is the Chairman of the Board of Governors of the Leader to Leader Institute and former CEO of the Girl Scouts of the USA. She was awarded the Presidential Medal of Freedom, the United States of America's highest civilian honor, in 1998. In 2002 she was the first recipient of the Dwight D. Eisenhower National Security Series Award for her service with the

U.S. Army in leadership development. She is author of *Hesselbein on Leadership*, published in August of 2002, and is the coeditor of 20 books in 28 languages.

John Hume is a principal architect of the peace process in Northern Ireland and was corecipient of the 1998 Nobel Prize for Peace. Cofounder of the Social Democratic and Labour Party, which he led from 1979 until 2001, he represented Northern Ireland in the European Parliament and the Foyle constituency in the House of Commons at Westminster. Earlier, he was elected as an independent member of the Northern Ireland Parliament. He currently holds the Tip O'Neill Chair in Peace Studies at the University of Ulster, where he continues to work for the cause of peace.

Erik R. Peterson is Senior Vice President at the Center for Strategic and International Studies (CSIS), the bipartisan and nonprofit think tank established in the nation's capital in 1962 to weigh policy options and solutions to the constellation of global challenges. He also is Director of the CSIS Global Strategy Institute, the mandate of which is to carry out analysis on long-term global trends, and holder of the William A. Schreyer Chair on Global Analysis.

Beheruz N. Sethna is President of The University of West Georgia, a 10,000-student comprehensive university where he also serves as Professor of Business Administration. A native of India, he is the first known person of Indian origin ever to serve as president of a university in the United States. He also has served in an interim capacity as Senior Vice Chancellor of the University System of Georgia, and as dean and member of faculty at several U.S. universities. A frequent speaker and media commentator, he is author of more than 50 scholarly articles and a book.

David J. Siegel is Associate Professor of Educational Leadership (higher education concentration) at East Carolina University. His research interests center on the changing role of colleges and universities in society, with a particular focus on interorganizational (academic-corporate-nonprofit) partnerships to address the challenges of diversity. He is the author of the book *The Call for Diversity* and journal articles exploring public–private collaborations in support of diversity-related objectives.

Michael J. Siegel is Assistant Professor and Director of the Administration of Higher Education Program at Suffolk University. Prior to joining the Suffolk faculty in 2005, he was Research Fellow at the Policy Center on the

First Year of College in North Carolina. He is the coauthor of the book *Achieving and Sustaining Institutional Excellence for the First Year of College* and author of *Primer on Assessment of the First College Year.*

David Whyte is an Associate Fellow at Templeton College and Said Business School at the University of Oxford, and one of the few poets to take his perspectives on creativity into the field of organizational development, where he works with many major companies. A well-known speaker and workshop leader, he is the author of five volumes of poetry and two additional books, *The Heart Aroused: Poetry and the Preservation of the Soul in Corporate America* and *Crossing the Unknown Sea: Work as a Pilgrimage of Identity.*

E.T. York is Chancellor Emeritus of the State University System of Florida and former Vice President for Agricultural Affairs and Interim President of the University of Florida. Prior to joining the University of Florida in 1963, he held positions including head of the Agronomy Department at North Carolina State University and Administrator of the Federal Extension Service. The author of more than 100 papers and books, he was appointed to prominent advisory positions by Presidents Kennedy, Johnson, Nixon, Ford, Carter, and Reagan; by various foreign governments; and by a number of U.S. government agencies. Since 1980, he has dedicated himself full-time to a wide range of activities related to the problems of world hunger and malnutrition.